Terrible Tsarinas

Henri Troyat
Member of the French Academy

Terrible Tsarinas

—

Five Russian Women
in Power

Translated by Andrea Lyn Secara

Algora Publishing
New York

Algora Publishing, New York
© 2001 by Algora Publishing
All rights reserved. Published 2001.
Printed in the United States of America
ISBN: 1-892941-54-6
Editors@algora.com

Originally published as *Terribles tsarines* © *Editions Grasset &*
Fasquelle, 1998.

Library of Congress Cataloging-in-Publication Data 2001-003133

Troyat, Henri, 1911-
  [Terribles tsarines. English]
  Terrible tsarinas : five Russian women in power / by Henri Troyat.
      p. cm.
  Includes bibliographical references and index.
  ISBN 1-892941-54-6 (alk. paper)
  1. Russia—History—1689-1801. 2. Russia—Kings and
Rulers—Biography. 3. Empresses—Russia—Biography. I. Title: Five
Russian women in power. II. Title.
  DK127 .T76613 2001
  947'.05'0922—dc21

                                                    2001003133

Algora Publishing
wishes to express appreciation
to the French Ministry of Culture
for its support
of this work through the
Centre National du livre.

New York
www.algora.com

Other Works by Henri Troyat

Individual Novels

FAUX JOUR (Plon)
LE VIVIER (Plon)
GRANDEUR NATURE (Plon)
L'ARAIGNE (Plon) — Prix Goncourt 1938
LE MORT SAISIT LE VIF (Plon)
LE SIGNE DU TAUREAU (Plon)
LA TÊTE SUR LES ÉPAULES (Plon)
UNE EXTRÊME AMITIÉ (La Table Ronde)
LA NEIGE EN DEUIL (Flammarion)
LA PIERRE, LA FEUILLE ET LES CISEAUX (Flammarion)
ANNE PRÉDAILLE (Flammarion)
GRIMBOSQ (Flammarion)
LE FRONT DANS LES NUAGES (Flammarion)
LE PRISONNIER No 1 (Flammarion)
LE PAIN DE L'ÉTRANGER (Flammarion)
LA DÉRISION (Flammarion)
MARIE KARPOVNA (Flammarion)
LE BRUIT SOLITAIRE DU CŒUR (Flammarion)
TOUTE MA VIE SERA MENSONGE (Flammarion)
LA GOUVERNANTE FRANÇAISE (Flammarion)
LA FEMME DE DAVID (Flammarion)
ALIOCHA (Flammarion)
YOURI (Flammarion)
LE CHANT DES INSENSÉS (Flammarion)
LE MARCHAND DE MASQUES (Flammarion)
LE DÉFI D'OLGA (Flammarion)
VOTRE TRÈS HUMBLE ET TRÈS OBÉISSANT SERVITEUR (Flammarion)
L'AFFAIRE CRÉMONNIÈRE (Flammarion)
LE FILS DU SATRAPE (Grasset)

Series of Novels

LES SEMAILLES ET LES MOISSONS (Plon)
LES HÉRITIERS DE L'AVENIR (Flammarion)
TANT QUE LA TERRE DURERA... (La Table Ronde)
LE MOSCOVITE (Flammarion)
VIOU (Flammarion)

Novellas

LA CLEF DE VOÛTE (Plon)
LA FOSSE COMMUNE (Plon)

LE JUGEMENT DE DIEU (Plon)
DU PHILANTHROPE À LA ROUQUINE (Flammarion)
LE GESTE D'ÈVE (Flammarion)
LES AILES DU DIABLE (Flammarion)

Biographies

DOSTOÏEVSKI (Fayard)
POUCHKINE (Perrin)
L'ÉTRANGE DESTIN DE LERMONTOV (Perrin)
TOLSTOÏ (Fayard)
GOGOL (Flammarion)
CATHERINE LA GRANDE (Flammarion)
PIERRE LE GRAND (Flammarion)
ALEXANDRE I (Flammarion)
IVAN LE TERRIBLE (Flammarion)
TCHEKHOV (Flammarion)
TOURGUENIEV (Flammarion)
GORKI (Flammarion)
FLAUBERT (Flammarion)
MAUPASSANT (Flammarion)
ALEXANDRE II (Flammarion)
NICOLAS II (Flammarion)
ZOLA (Flammarion)
VERLAINE (Flammarion)
BAUDELAIRE (Flammarion)
BALZAC (Flammarion)
RASPOUTINE (Flammarion)
JULIETTE DROUET (Flammarion)

Essays, Travel and Other Writings

LA CASE DE L'ONCLE SAM (La Table Ronde)
DE GRATTE-CIEL EN COCOTIER (Plon)
SAINTE-RUSSIE, réflexions et souvenirs (Grasset)
LES PONTS DE PARIS, illustré d'aquarelles (Flammarion)
NAISSANCE D'UNE DAUPHINE (Gallimard)
LA VIE QUOTIDIENNE EN RUSSIE AU TEMPS DU DERNIER TSAR (Hachette)
LES VIVANTS, théâtre (André Bonne)
UN SI LONG CHEMIN (Stock)

CONTENTS

I

CATHERINE SHOWS THE WAY

A despondent hush fell upon the Winter Palace. While the stupor that marks the death of a sovereign is usually followed of an outburst of joy when the name of the successor is proclaimed, this time the minutes ticked by and the courtiers' dejection, their uncertainty, stretched until the verge of alarm. It was as though Peter the Great were still dying. Some people even seemed to think that, without him, Russia had no future. Contemplating the enormous corpse, its hands clasped and eyes shut forever, all the notables who had come running at the news were astonished that this man of monstrous energy and audacity, who had pried the country out of its age-old lethargy and provided it with an administration, a police force, and an army worthy of a modern power, who had sloughed off the weight of Russian traditions and opened the nation to Western culture, and built a capital of endless splendor on a wasteland of mud and water, had not taken the trouble to name a successor.

It is true that, even a few months before, there had been nothing to suggest that he might meet such a sudden demise. As usual, the reformist tsar had fallen victim to his own impetuosity. Diving into the icy waters of the Neva to rescue sailors from a sinking ship, he contracted the pneumonia that was to carry him off. The fever very quickly triggered the after-effects of his venereal disease, with complications including gangrene, gravel in the kidneys, and retention of urine. January 28, 1725, after painful days of delirium, he called for writing materials and, with a trembling hand, traced on the paper the words: "Pass everything on to. . ." The name of the beneficiary was left blank. The failing fingers were already contracting, and his voice trailed off in a death rattle. He was gone.

Collapsing at his bedside, his wife Catherine sobbed and queried the mute, deaf and inert body — in vain. This instantaneous bereavement left her both desperate and disabled, weighing her down with a grief and an empire that were equally crushing. All around her, every thoughtful person in the realm shared the same anguish. In reality, despotism is an indispensable drug not only to the one who exerts it but to those who are subjected to it, as well. The megalomania of the master is matched by the masochism of the subjects. People who have become accustomed to the injustices of a policy of force are frightened when it is abruptly removed. They feel as though the master (whom they had just been complaining about), in loosening his embrace, has withdrawn at the same time his protection and his love. Those who used to quietly criticize the tsar now did not know which foot to dance on. They even wondered whether this was the time to "dance" at all, and whether they would "dance" again some day, after this long wait in the shadow of the tyrannical innovator.

However, life must go on, whatever the cost. While shedding copious tears, Catherine kept sight of her personal interests. A widow can be sincerely afflicted and at the same time reasonably ambitious. She was quite aware of the times she had wronged the recently departed, but she had always remained devoted to him in spite of her many infidelities. No one had known him and served him better than she throughout the 23 years of their relationship and marriage. In the struggle for power, she had — if not dynastic legitimacy — then at least disinterested love going for her.

Among the dignitaries close to the throne, the bets were already open. Who would win the crown of Monomakh?[1] Within a few feet of the corpse laid out on the ceremonial bier, they were whispering, plotting, and proffering one name or another — without daring to declare out loud their own preferences. Some were partisans of young Peter, ten years old, the son of the poor tsarevich Alexis. (Peter the Great had had Alexis tortured to death to punish him for allegedly having plotted against him.) The memory of this legal assassination still hovered like smoke over the Russian court. The coterie loyal to young Peter included the princes Dmitri Golitsyn, Ivan Dolgoruky, Nikita Repnin, and Boris Sheremetiev, all displeased with having been persecuted by the tsar and avid to take their revenge under the new reign. In the other corner were those known as "Peter the Great's Fledglings." His Majesty's right-hand men, they were always on the alert to preserve their prerogatives. At their head stood Alexander Menshikov, a former pastry-cook's helper, a childhood friend and favorite of the deceased (who had promoted him to Serene Prince), Ivan Buturlin, a lieutenant-colonel of the Guard, the senator Count Peter Tolstoy, Grand Chancellor Count Gabriel Golovkin, and the Lord High Admiral Fyodor Apraxin. To please Peter the Great, all these high-ranking individuals had signed the High Court's verdict condemning to torture, and consequently to death, his rebellious son Alexis. For Catherine, these men represented a group of allies of unshakeable fidelity. These "men of progress," who were outspokenly hostile toward the retrograde ideas of the old aristocracy, had no hesitation: only Peter's widow had the right and the ability to succeed him.

Of the men who were determined to defend the cause of "the true guardian of the imperial thought" the most devoted was the one who had the most to gain — the dashing Alexander Menshikov. He owed his entire career to the tsar's friendship, and he counted on the gratitude of the wife to maintain his privileges. His conviction was so strong that he would not even hear of Peter the Great's grandson's claims to the crown; certainly, he was the son of the tsarevich Alexis, but nothing, except that coincidence of family, destined him to such a glorious fate. Similarly, he shrugged off the pretensions of the daughters of Peter the Great and Catherine who could, after all, also present their candidatures. The elder of the two daughters, Anna Petrovna, was just seventeen years old; the junior, Elizabeth Petrovna, was barely sixteen. Neither one was particularly dangerous. In any event, according to the order of the succession, they would only come after their mother, the putative empress. For the moment, the priority was to get them married as quickly as possible. Catherine was quite unconcerned about that and relied on Menshikov and his friends to support her in her intrigues. Before the tsar had even heaved his last sigh, they sent emissaries to the principal barracks to prepare the officers of the Guard for a coup d'état in favor of their future "little mother Catherine."

As the doctors and then the priests recorded the death of Peter the Great, a wan sunrise seeped over the sleeping city. It was snowing, with great soft flakes. Catherine wrung her hands and wept so abundantly in front of the plenipotentiaries assembled around the funeral bed that Captain Villebois, Peter the Great's aide-de-camp, would note in his memoirs: "One could not conceive that there could be so much water in a woman's brain. Many people ran to the palace just to see her crying and sighing."[2]

The tsar's death was finally announced by a 100-gun salute fired from the Peter and Paul fortress. The bells tolled on every church. It was time to make a decision. The whole nation was waiting to find out whom it would have to adore — or fear — in the future. At eight o'clock in the morning, conscious of her responsibility before History, Catherine proceeded to a large hall in the palace where the senators were gathered, with the members of Holy Synod and the dignitaries of the first four classes of the hierarchy — a sort of Council of the Wise known as the "Generalité" of the empire.

The discussion was impassioned from the start. To begin with, Peter the Great's personal secretary Makarov swore on the Gospels that the tsar had not written a will. Seizing the ball on the rebound, Menshikov pleaded eloquently on behalf of His Majesty's widow. His first argument was that, having married the former maidservant from Livonia (Catherine was born Marta Skawronska) in 1707, Peter the Great had then chosen, one year before his death, to have her crowned empress in the Cathedral of the Archangel, in Moscow. By this solemn and unprecedented act, according to Menshikov, he had shown that there was no need to resort to any written will since, while he was alive, Peter had taken care to bless his wife as sole inheritor of power.

But this explanation struck his adversaries as specious: they objected that in no monarchy in the world did the crowning of the monarch's wife confer upon her *ipso facto* the right to the succession. Supporting this viewpoint, Prince Dmitri Golitsyn advanced the candidature of the sovereign's grandson, Peter Alexeyevich, the proper son of Alexis — saying that this child, of the same blood as the deceased, should be considered before all the other applicants. However, given the boy's tender age, that choice would imply the designation of a regent until he came of majority; and every regency in Russia had been marred by conspiracies and disturbances. The latest, centered around the Grand Duchess Sophia, had nearly compromised the reign of her brother Peter the Great. She had woven against him intrigues so black that she had had to be thrown into a convent to stop her wicked ways. Did the nobles want to go through that kind of experience again, by bringing to power their protégé, with a guardian hovering over him and offering advice? The adversaries in this party suggested that women are not prepared to direct the affairs of an empire as vast as Russia. Their nerves, they said, are too fragile, and they are surrounded by greedy favorites whose extravagances are far too costly to the nation. With that, the supporters of young Peter asserted that Catherine was a woman like Sophia and that it was better to have an imperfect regent than an inexperienced empress. Stung by the affront, Menshikov and Tolstoy reminded the critics that Catherine had demonstrated an almost virile courage in following her husband to every battlefield and had shown a well-trained mind in her covert participation in all his political decisions. When the debate was at its hottest, murmurs of approval rose from the back of the room. Several officers of the Guard had infiltrated the assembly (without being invited), and they delivered their opinion on a question which, in theory, concerned only the members of the Generalité.

General Repnin, outraged by this impertinence, sought to drive out the intruders, but Ivan Buturlin had already gone up to a window and was moving his hand in a queer way. At this signal, drum rolls resounded from afar, accompanied by fifes playing martial music. Two regiments of the Guard, convened in haste, were waiting in an inner court of the palace for the order to intervene. While they noisily penetrated the building, Repnin, crimson-faced, howled: "Who dared. . . without my orders. . . ?" "I followed those of Her Majesty, the Empress," answered Buturlin, without leaving the window.

This demonstration by the army stifled the last of the protesters' exclamations. In the meantime, Catherine had slipped away. She had been sure of her victory from the first comments. In the presence of the troops, the Lord High Admiral Apraxin had Makarov confirm that no will existed that opposed the assembly's decision and, thus reassured, he concluded goodnaturedly, "Let us go and offer our homage to the reigning empress!" The best arguments are those of the saber and the gun. Convinced in the wink of an eye, the Generalité, princes, senators, generals and ecclesiastics submissively moved toward the apartments of Her very new Majesty.

In order to conform to legal procedures, Menshikov and Buturlin promulgated a proclamation that same day certifying that "the very serene Prince Peter the Great, emperor and sovereign of all the Russias," had wished to regulate the succession of the empire by having "his dear wife, our very gracious Empress and Dame Catherine Alexeyevna [crowned], . . . because of the great and important services that she has rendered to the advantage of the Russian Empire. . . ." At the bottom of the proclamation one may read, "Presented to the Senate, in St. Petersburg, January 28, 1725."[3]

The publication of this document aroused no serious opposition among the notables nor the general public; and Catherine began to breathe more easily. The deal was done. For her, it was a second birth. When she thought back to her past as a soldiers' whore, she was dizzied by her elevation to the rank of legitimate wife, then of sovereign. Her parents, simple Livonian farmers, had died of the plague one after the other, when she was still very young. After wandering through the countryside, famished and all in tatters, she was taken in by the Lutheran pastor Glück, who employed her as a maidservant. But, an orphan with a tempting figure, she quickly betrayed his tutelage and ran off, sleeping in the camps of the Russian army that had come to conquer Polish Livonia. She rose in rank from one lover to another, until she became the mistress of Menshikov, then of Peter himself. If he enjoyed her, it was certainly not for her education, for she was practically illiterate and she spoke execrable Russian; but he had many occasions to appreciate her valiancy, her spirit and her great allure. The tsar had always sought out women who were well-endowed in flesh and simple in spirit. Even if Catherine was often untrue to him, even if he was fed up with her betrayals, he returned to her even after the worst quarrels. The notion that the "break up" was final, this time, left her feeling both punished and relieved.

The fate that was in store for her seemed extraordinary, not only because of her modest origins but because of her gender, which historically had been relegated to secondary roles. No woman before her had ever been empress of Russia. From time immemorial, the throne of that immense land had been occupied by males, according to the hereditary line of descent. Even after the death of Ivan the Terrible and the confusion that followed, neither the impostor Boris Godunov nor the shaky Fyodor II nor the theory of the false Dmitris that plagued the "Time of Troubles" had changed anything in the monarchical tradition of virility.

It took the extinction of the house of Rurik, the founder of old Russia, for the country to resign itself to having a tsar elected by an assembly of boyars, prelates and dignitaries (the "Sobor"). Young Mikhail Fyodorovich, the first of the Romanovs, was chosen. After him, imperial power was transmitted without too many clashes for nearly a century. It was only in 1722 that Peter the Great, breaking with tradition, decreed that the sovereign should thenceforth designate an heir however seemed best to him, without regard for the dynastic order. Thus, thanks to this innovator who had already upset his country's ways from top to bottom, a woman of no birth or political qualification had the same rights as a man to assume the throne. And the first to benefit from this inordinate privilege would be a former servant, a Livonian by origin and a Protestant at that, who became Russian and Orthodox late in the game and whose only claims to glory were acquired in the sack. Is it possible that the hands that had so often washed the dishes, made the beds, bleached the dirty linen and prepared the swill for the army rabble would be the same ones that tomorrow, scented and bearing rings, would sign the *ukases* upon which hung the future of million subjects, frozen with respect and fear?

Day and night, the idea of this formidable promotion haunted Catherine's mind. The more she wept, the more she felt like laughing. Official mourning was to go on for forty days. All the ladies of quality vied in prayers and lamentations; Catherine held her own superbly in this contest of sighing and sobbing. But suddenly, another grief struck her heart. Four weeks after the demise of her husband, while the entire city was preparing his sumptuous funeral, her younger daughter Natalya (six and a half years old) succumbed to measles. This inconspicuous, almost insignificant death, coming on top of the tremendous impact of the death of Peter the Great, fully convinced Catherine that her fate was exceptional, in suffering as well as in success. She immediately decided to bury on the same day the father, wreathed in glory of historic proportions, and the little girl who had never had time to taste the happiness and the constraints of a woman's life. Announced by heralds at the four corners of the capital, the double funeral was to take place on March 10, 1725, in the Cathedral of SS Peter and Paul.

All along the route of the procession, the façades of the houses were draped in black. Twelve colonels of high stature bore His Majesty's imposing coffin, which was sheltered to some extent from the gusts of snow and hail by a canopy of gilt brocade and green velvet. Natalya's little coffin accompanied it under a canopy of gilt fabric decorated with plumes of red and white feathers. Behind them the priests advanced, preceding a host of sacred banners and icons. Finally came Catherine I, in deep mourning, her gaze lowered. The inevitable Serene Prince Menshikov and the Lord High Admiral Apraxin supported her faltering steps. Her daughters Anna and Elizabeth were escorted by the Grand Chancellor Golovkin, General Repnin and Count Tolstoy. All the highest dignitaries, the greatest members of the nobility, the most decorated generals, and the foreign princes and diplomats who were visiting the court, followed the cortege, arranged according to seniority, heads bared, treading to the rhythm of funeral music punctuated with drum rolls. The guns thundered, the bells tolled, the wind caught at the wigs of the high and mighty — who had to hold onto them with their hands. After two hours of walking in the cold and the storm, the arrival at the church seemed like a deliverance. The immense cathedral suddenly looked too small to contain this exhausted and tear-stained crowd. And then, in the nave illuminated by thousands of candles, another torment began. The liturgy was crushingly slow. Catherine called on all her reserves of energy not to weaken. With equal fervor, she bade farewell to the prestigious husband who had made her a gift of Russia and to the innocent child whom she would never again see smiling as she awoke from sleep.

But, if Natalya's death wrung her heart like the sight of a bird fallen from the nest, that of Peter exalted her like an invitation to the astonishments of a legendary destiny. Born to be last, she had become first. Whom should she thank for this fortune, God or her husband? Or both, according to the circumstances? Plunged into this solemn interrogation, she heard the voice of the archbishop of Pskov, Feofan (Theophanes) Prokopovich, pronouncing the funeral oration. "What has befallen us, O men of

Russia? What are we seeing? What are we doing? It is Peter the Great whom we are burying!" And, in conclusion, this comforting prophecy: "Russia will go on as he molded it!"

At these words, Catherine raised her head. She had no doubt that, in uttering this sentence, the priest was transmitting a message to her from beyond the tomb. By turns exalted and frightened at the prospect of the days to come, she found herself stifling in the crowd. But, exiting the church, she found the square looked vaster, emptier, more inhospitable than before. The snow was coming down harder. Even though flanked by her daughters and friends, Catherine felt acutely alone, lost in an unknown land. It was as though the absence of Peter had paralyzed her. It would take all her courage to face the reality of a Russia with no future and no master.

Footnotes

1. According to legend, Monomakh's Cap (the oldest crown in the Russian treasury) was a gift from the Byzantine emperor Constantine IX Monomachus to his grandson Vladimir II Monomakh, grand prince of Kiev (1113-1125).
2. Villebois: *Mémoires secrets pour servir à l'histoire de la cour de Russie.*
3. In the 18th century, Russia was still using the Gregorian calendar, so that this date is 11 days behind the date shown by the Julian calendar currently in use.

II

CATHERINE'S REIGN: A FLASH OF FLAMBOYANCE

Catherine I was almost fifty. She had lived so much, loved so much, laughed so much, drunk so much — but she was never satisfied. Those who knew her during this period of ostentatious pleasure described her as a large, rotund woman, heavily made up, smiling, with a triple chin, a ribald eye and gluttonous lips, garishly dressed, overloaded with jewels and not necessarily entirely clean.

However, while everyone denounced her appearance as a camp-follower masquerading as a sovereign, opinions are more varied when it comes to her intelligence and decision-making ability. She barely knew how to read and write; she barely spoke Russian (and with a Swedish-tinged Polish accent, at that); but from the first days of her reign she displayed a creditable intention to emulate her husband's thinking. She even learned a little French and German in order to improve her understanding of foreign policy issues. And she relied on the common sense that she inherited from a difficult childhood. Some of her interlocutors found her more human, more understanding than the late tsar.

That being said, she was conscious of her lack of experience and consulted Menshikov before making any important decision. Her enemies claimed, behind her back, that she was entirely beholden to him and that she was afraid of dissatisfying him through any personal initiative.

Was she still sleeping with him? Even if she had never deprived herself of that pleasure in the past, it is unlikely that she would have persevered at her age and in her situation. Avid for fair and flourishing flesh, she had no need to restrict herself to the pleasures that may be available in the arms of an aging partner. With complete freedom to choose, she changed lovers according to her fantasies and did not spare any expense when it came to rewarding them for their nights of prowess. The French ambassador, Jacques de Campredon, enjoyed enumerating some of these transitory darlings in his *Memoirs*: "Menshikov is no longer anything but an advisor," he writes. "Count Loewenwolde appears to have more credit. Sir Devier is still among the most outstanding favorites. Count Sapieha has also stepped up to the job. He is a fine young man, well-built. He is often sent bouquets and jewels. . . . There are other, second-class favorites, but they are known only to Johanna, a former chambermaid of the tsarina and agent of her pleasures."

At the many suppers she held to regale her companions in these tournaments of love, Catherine drank like a sailor. At her command, ordinary vodka (*prostaya*) was alternated, on the table, with strong French and German liquors. She quite often passed out at the end of these well-lubricated meals. "The tsarina was rather ill from one of these debaucheries that was held on St. Andrew's Day," noted the same Campredon in a report to his minister, dated December 25, 1725. "A bleeding set her up again; but, as she is extremely plump and lives so very irregularly, it is expected that she will have some accident that will shorten her days."[1]

These binges of drinking and lovemaking did not prevent Catherine from conducting herself like a true autocrat whenever she recovered her wits. She scolded and slapped her maidservants for a peccadillo, bellowed at her ordinary advisers, and attended without a misstep the tiresome parades of the Guard; she rode on horseback for hours at a time, to soothe her nerves and to prove to one and all that her physical stamina was beyond dispute. Since she had a sense of family, she brought in brothers and sisters (whose existence Peter the Great had always chosen to ignore) from their remote provinces. At her invitation, former Livonian and Lithuanian peasants, uncouth and awkwardly stuffed into formal clothing, disembarked in the salons of St. Petersburg. Titles of "Count" and "Prince" rained down on their heads, to the great scandal of the authentic aristocrats. Some of these new courtiers with calloused hands joined the rest of Her Majesty's dinner crowd in the conclaves of good humor and licentiousness.

Nonetheless, however keen she may have been for this disso-lute debauchery, Catherine always set aside a few hours to deal with public affairs. Certainly, Menshikov continued to dictate decisions in matters affecting the interests of the State, but, from one week to another, Catherine gained in confidence and began to stand up to her mentor, sometimes to the point of disputing his opinions.

While recognizing that she would never be able to do with-out the advice of this competent, devoted, wily man, she con-vinced him to convene around her a High Privy Council, including not only Menshikov but several other characters whose fidelity to Her Majesty was notorious: Tolstoy, Apraxin, Vice Chancellor Golovkin, Ostermann. . . This supreme cabinet relegated the tra-ditional Senate to the sidelines, where they no longer discussed any questions of primary importance. It was at the instigation of the High Council that Catherine decided to ease the fate of the

Old Believers, who were persecuted for their heretical beliefs; to create an Academy of Sciences according to the desires of Peter the Great; to accelerate the beautification of the capital; to pursue the construction of the Ladoga Canal; and to equip the expedition of Danish navigator Vitus Behring, who was bound for Kamchatka. These wise resolutions mixed oddly in the tsarina's turbulent mind with her penchant for sex and alcohol. She was voracious and well-disciplined by turn, hotly sensual and coldly lucid.

Hardly had she tasted the complementary joys of power and pleasure when she again turned her attention to her paramount concern: that of the family. Any mother, tsarina or not, considers it her mission to see her daughters established as soon as they reach the age of puberty. Catherine had given life to two pretty daughters, who were clever-minded enough to be as pleasing in their conversation as they were to look at. The elder, Anna Petrovna, had recently been promised to the duke of Holstein-Gottorp, Charles Frederick. Weak, nervous and ungainly, he had little but his title to attract the girl. But reason can overrule feelings when, beyond the union of the hearts, political alliances and territorial annexations are foreseen. The marriage having been delayed by Peter the Great's death, Catherine planned to celebrate it on May 21, 1725. Subservient to the maternal will, Anna sadly resigned herself to what she must have seen as her only choice. She was 17 years old. Charles Frederick was 25. The archbishop Feofan Prokopovich, who just a few weeks before had celebrated the funeral offices of Peter the Great in Old Slavonic, the language of the Church, now blessed the union of the daughter of the deceased with the son of Duke Frederick of Holstein and Hedwige of Sweden, herself daughter of King Charles XI. As the fiancé spoke neither Slavonic nor Russian, an interpreter translated the key passages into Latin for him.

The party was entertained by the acrobatics and contortions of a pair of dwarves, who spouted out of an enormous meat pie while dessert was being brought in. The attendees choked with laughter and burst into applause. The bride herself enjoyed it. She did not suspect the bitter disappointment that awaited her. Three day after the wedding ceremony, the Saxon diplomatic representative let his king know that Charles Frederick had stayed out all night three times in a row, leaving Anna fretting alone in her bed. "The mother is in despair at her daughter's sacrifice," he wrote in his report. A little later he would add that the scorned wife was comforting herself "by spending the night with one and another."[2]

While regretting her elder daughter's poor luck, Catherine refused to admit defeat and sought to interest her son-in-law in public affairs — since he appeared so little interested in private affairs. She guessed correctly: Charles Frederick was mad about politics. Invited to participate in the meetings of the Supreme Privy Council, he threw himself into the debates with so much passion that Catherine was alarmed, finding that he sometimes meddled in matters that were not his concern.

Dissatisfied with this first son-in-law, she thought to correct her mistake by arranging a marriage that all of Europe would envy for her second daughter, Elizabeth, who had been Peter the Great's preferred. Europe was known to her mostly through the remarks of her late husband and, recently, through her diplomats' reports. But, while Peter the Great had found the Germanic rigor, discipline and efficiency attractive, Catherine found the charms and the spirit of France increasingly appealing. She heard wonderful tales from all who visited Paris — they claimed that the pomp and ceremonies of the court at Versailles were incomparable in their refinement. Some went as far as to say that the elegance and intelligence that the French people prided themselves on added luster to the enlightened authority of its government and the power of its army.

The French ambassador, Jacques de Campredon, often spoke to Catherine of the benefits that a rapprochement would represent between two countries that had every reason to support each other. According to him, such an agreement would relieve the empress of the underhanded interventions of England, which never missed an opportunity to interfere in Russia's disputes with Turkey, Denmark, Sweden and Poland. For the four years that this distinguished diplomat played his role in St. Petersburg, he never stopped his sly preaching in favor of a Franco-Russian alliance. From his first days at the court, he had alerted his minister, Cardinal Dubois, that the tsar's younger daughter, little Elizabeth Petrovna ("very pleasant and good-looking") would be an excellent wife for a prince of the house of France. But, at the time, the Regent favored the English and feared irritating them by expressing any interest in a Russian grand duchess. The tenacious Campredon now returned to his original thought. Couldn't the negotiations that had been broken off with the tsar be taken up again, after his death, with the tsarina?

Campredon sought to persuade his government that they could and, to prepare the ground, he redoubled his attentions towards Catherine. The empress was flattered, in her maternal pride, by the admiration the diplomat expressed for her daughter. Wasn't this, she thought, a premonitory sign of the warm sentiments that all the French would one day feel for Russia? With emotion, she remembered Peter the Great's fondness for little Elizabeth, so young then, so blonde, so slender, so playful. The gamine was only seven years old when Peter asked the French painter Caravaque, a familiar figure at the palace in St. Petersburg, to paint her in the nude so that he could look at her at any hour, whenever he wished. He certainly would have been very proud to have his child, so beautiful and so virtuous, selected for marriage by a great prince of France. A few months after her husband's funeral, Catherine showed herself receptive to Campredon's suggestions. Matrimonial discussions were thus picked up again at the point where they had been dropped upon the death of the tsar.

In April 1725, the rumor spread that the *infanta* Maria Anna (the 7-year-old daughter of King Philip V of Spain), who was supposed to have been engaged to the 15-year-old Louis XV, was about to be sent back to her country because the French regent, the Duke of Bourbon,[3] considered her too young for the role. Inspired, Catherine called for Campredon; he could only confirm the news.

Catherine then waxed sympathetic over the fate of the unfortunate *infanta*, but declared that the regent's decision did not surprise her, for one cannot play with impunity with the sacred candor of childhood. Then, wary of Naryshkin, the grand master of the court who was present during this meeting, she went on in Swedish. Praising Elizabeth's physical and moral qualities, she stressed the importance that the grand duchess would have on the international chessboard in the case of a family accord with France. She did not dare to state her thoughts outright, opting merely to assert, with a prophetic gleam in her eyes: "We would prefer friendship and an alliance with the King of France over all the other princes in the world." Her dream: that her dear little Elizabeth, "that little royal morsel," should become Queen of France. How many problems would be resolved smoothly, from one end of Europe to the other, if Louis XV agreed to become her son-in-law! If need be, she promised, the fiancée would adopt the Catholic religion. This offer struck Campredon very much like a declaration of love; he dissolved in thanks and asked to be given time to transmit the details of the proposal to his superiors. For his part, Menshikov went to the ambassador and swore to him that Elizabeth's intelligence and grace were "worthy of the French

genius," that "she was born for France" and that she would dazzle
Versailles from her first appearance at the court. Persuaded that
the Regent would not be able to withstand these arguments, dictated by sincere friendship, he went even further and suggested
supplementing the marriage of Louis XV and Elizabeth by marrying the Duke of Bourbon with Maria Leszczynska, the daughter of
King Stanislaw of Poland, who was currently exiled in Wissem-
bourg. Indeed, someday this deposed sovereign might find his
way to the throne, if Russia did not find it too disadvantageous.

Secret memoranda went back and forth between the chancelleries for three months. To Catherine's great surprise, no reso-
lution seemed to be forthcoming from the French. Could they
have misplayed their hand? Would they have to consider other
concessions, other compromises in order to take the top prize?
Catherine was lost in conjecture, in September 1725, when the
news broke like a thunderclap in the misty skies over St. Petersburg: confounding all predictions, Louis XV would marry Maria
Leszczynska, the empty-handed 22-year-old Pole, whom the Empress of Russia had thought of offering as a token to the Duke of
Bourbon.

This announcement was a superb snub to the tsarina. Outraged, she ordered Menshikov to discover the reasons behind such
a misalliance. He caught up with Campredon on his way to an
appointment between seconds, preliminary to a meeting of the
sword. Pressed with questions, the diplomat tried to hedge, fell
into rambling explanations, spoke of reciprocal inclinations between the fiancés (which seemed somewhat implausible), and
ended up implying that the House of France was not lacking in
applicants with whom the pretty Elizabeth might be satisfied, in
the absence of a king. Certain princes, he insinuated, would be
better partners than the sovereign himself.

Clutching the last hope that was offered, Catherine, disappointed by Louis XV, decided to try for the Duke of Charolais. This time, she thought, no one could accuse them of aiming too high. Informed of this haggling, Elizabeth's pride was hurt and she begged her mother to give up her ill-considered ambitions, which dishonored them both. However, Catherine claimed to know better than anyone else what would be good for her daughter. Although she believed she was finally betting on a winning horse, she suddenly ran into an even more humiliating refusal. "Monseigneur is pledged to another," declared Campredon, with pained courtesy. The ambassador was truly distressed by the series of affronts that he was charged with inflicting upon the empress. The court of Russia was becoming unbearable to him. He was ready to leave his post. But his minister, the Count de Morville, enjoined him to remain in place, warding off, on the one hand, debates over Elizabeth's marriage prospects and, on the other hand, any attempt to bring together St. Petersburg with Vienna. This double responsibility worried the prudent Campredon. He no longer understood his country's erratic political course. Learning that Catherine had invited the High Council to break off relations with France, which clearly wanted nothing to do with her, and to prepare an offensive and defensive alliance with Austria (which was disposed to help Russia, come what may), the diplomat — disappointed, cheated, and sick at heart — demanded his passports and on March 31, 1726, left the banks of the Neva, never more to return.

After his departure, Catherine felt like someone who has been misled in a youthful love affair. France, whom she adored so much, had rejected her and betrayed her for another. It was not her daughter who had been spurned, it was she, with her scepter, her crown, her army, the glorious history of her fatherland and her disproportionate hopes. Wounded to the quick, she sent a representative to Vienna with the charge to negotiate the alliance that she had so often refused. From now on, Europe would be divided into two camps: Russia, Austria and Spain on one side; France, England, Holland and Prussia on the other. . . Certainly, the lines might shift and influences might be felt across the borders, but, overall, in Catherine's eyes, the map was now drawn for the years to come.

Amidst all this diplomatic intrigue, her advisers clashed, making proposals and counter-proposals, haggling, arguing and reconciling. Since joining the Supreme Privy Council, Duke Charles Frederick of Holstein had distinguished himself by the boldness of his demands. His need to regain possession of the territories that once belonged to his family had turned into an obsession. He viewed all the history of the globe through that of the tiny duchy that he claimed was still his prerogative. Aggravated by his continual claims, Catherine finally made an official request to the King of Denmark to return Schleswig to her son-in-law, the Grand Duke of Holstein-Gottorp. Encountering a categorical refusal on behalf of the Danish sovereign, Frederick IV, she called upon the friendship of Austria and obtained its support for the gadfly Charles Frederick's claims to that parcel of land that, so recently, had been part of his heritage and that he so shamefully had been deprived of by the treaties of Stockholm and Frederiksborg. England then weighed in, making this imbroglio all the more delicate.

The more vexing these knotty foreign affairs issues became, the more the tsarina resorted to her favorite solace, drink. But, far from relieving her torment, the excesses at the table began to undermine her health. She stayed up partying until nine o'clock in the morning and collapsed, drunk dead, on her bed, in the arms of a partner whom she hardly recognized. The reverberations of this disorderly existence dismayed her entourage. The courtiers began to murmur among themselves, predicting the destruction of the monarchy.

As if the sempiternal gossip were not enough to poison the atmosphere at the palace, now people began talking again about that imp of a grandson of Peter the Great, whom they insisted had been wrongfully shunted aside. Issue of the unfortunate Alexis, who had paid with his life for having the audacity to oppose the policies of "The Reformer," he was staggered to learn that his name had cropped up in the debates over the succession. The innocent's adversaries maintained that he must share the paternal forfeiture and that he was permanently excluded from the prerogatives of the dynasty. But others claimed that his rights to the crown were inalienable and that he was very much in a position to mount the throne. . . under the tutelage of his close relations. His partisans were recruited primarily among the old stock nobility and the members of the provincial clergy.

Here and there, spontaneous uprisings were beginning to be seen in the countryside. Nothing serious, yet: timid gatherings in front of churches, secret meetings at the end of mass, the name of young Peter proclaimed by the crowds during festivals on his name day. Chancellor Ostermann, seeking to defuse the threat of a coup d'état, suggested marrying the tsarevich (who was not yet 12 years old) to his aunt Elizabeth, aged 17. No one bothered to consider whether that arrangement would suit the interested parties. Even Catherine, usually so sensitive to the inclinations of the heart, did not stop to ask herself what kind of future might await the couple that, at her initiative, would be formed by a scarcely pubescent boy and a young woman already going to seed. However, while the age difference hardly struck the unrepentant matchmakers as an insurmountable obstacle, they recognized that the Church was likely to oppose this consanguineous union. After long discussions, the idea was put aside. Moreover, Menshikov had a better suggestion. With self-serving audacity, he now suggested having tsarevich Peter marry not Elizabeth, but his own daughter, Maria Alexandrovna, who — according to him — combined beauty of the soul and that of the body. If he married her, Peter would be the happiest of men.

Admittedly, since 1721 she had been promised to Peter Sapieha, palatine of Smolensk, and she was said to be madly in love with her fiancé. But that detail did not stop Catherine. If everyone's feelings were taken into account before asking for the blessing of a priest, no one would ever marry anybody! The tsarina abruptly decided to break the engagement of these turtle doves, since it stood in the way of her wishes, and to marry the tsarevich Peter Alexeyevich and the young Maria Alexandrovna Menshikov. In compensation, Peter Sapieha would be offered one of Her Majesty's great-nieces, Sophia Skavronska. Meanwhile, moreover, Sapieha had been admitted to the very accessible bed of Catherine, on several occasions, and she was thus able to verify the virile qualities of the man she intended for her young relative. Sapieha, who knew how to get along in life, did not protest against the switch in fiancées; Catherine and Menshikov were pleased to think they had settled the matter so handily. Only the unfortunate Maria Alexandrovna was left to cry over her lost love and to curse her rival, Sophia Skavronska.

At the other end of the business, Anna and her husband, Duke Charles Frederick of Holstein, were equally dismayed by the possibility of a marriage that, under the pretext of promoting the interests of Peter Alexeyevich, would in fact serve to reinforce the hegemony of his future father-in-law, Menshikov, and would put even more distance between the throne and Peter the Great's two daughters. Considering themselves to have been sacrificed, but for different reasons, Anna and Elizabeth threw themselves at their mother's feet and begged her to give up the idea of this scandalous engagement that, all things considered, was satisfactory only to the instigator, the devious Menshikov. His sworn enemy, Count Tolstoy, supported them in their recriminations; he was enraged at the notion that he would see his direct competitor institutionalizing his authority by marrying his daughter to the heir to the Russian crown. Catherine appeared to be disturbed by this chorus of lamentations, and promised to think things over; she dismissed everyone without having made the least decision nor having made the least promise.

Time went by and Anna's and Elizabeth's consternation grew greater by the day, while Duke Charles Frederick of Holstein found less and less tolerable the arrogance shown by Menshikov, who felt sure of his imminent victory. People in the city were already talking, openly, about the impending marriage of the tsarevich with the noble and beautiful young lady, Maria Menshikov. And quietly, they were saying that the father of the intended had received fabulous sums from various people who were anxious to secure his protection in the years to come. Some, however, remembered that just a few months before, following a temporary illness, the worried tsarina had implied that after her death it was her younger daughter, Elizabeth, who should inherit the crown. This wish now seemed to have been forgotten completely. Elizabeth was upset by her mother's apparent repudiation but, being of a reserved nature, she forbore to counterattack. Her brother-in-law Duke Charles Frederick was less accommodating. Although the cause appeared desperate, he intended to fight to the end for Anna and himself. Come what may, he wanted to extract from his mother-in-law a will in favor of his wife.

However, by now Catherine was too weak to entertain such an unsettling discussion. Secluded in her apartments in the Winter Palace, she had difficulty speaking and even putting together her thoughts. Behind her back, it was whispered that Her Majesty's premature senility was the price to be paid for her excesses

in food, drink and lovemaking. Johann Lefort, Saxony's top diplomat in St. Petersburg, wrote to his government on March 8, 1727,
in picturesque and suggestive French: "The Tsarina apparently is
suffering a severe attack of swelling of the legs, all the way up to
the groin, which cannot bode well; this [ailment] is considered to
be of bacchic origins."[4] Despite of the doctor's warnings, Catherine's son-in-law baited her with questions regarding her intentions. But she was unable to answer him, nor even to understand
him. On April 27, 1729, she complained of a painful pressure in
the chest. Her eyes were wild, and she became delirious. Having
taken a cold look at her, Charles Frederick called in Tolstoy:

"If she passes away without having dictated her will, we are
lost! Can't we persuade her to designate her daughter, immediately?"

"If we have not already done so, it is too late now!"[5] the other
answered.

The empress's friends and family members watched for 48
hours, waiting for her to draw her last breath. Her daughters and
Peter Sapieha were at the bedside. She would hardly regain consciousness when the blackouts returned, longer each time and
more profound. Menshikov was kept current, hour by hour, on
the state of the tsarina. He convoked the Supreme Privy Council
and set about drafting a testamentary proclamation that the Empress would only have to sign, a mere little bit of scribble, before
dying. Under the authority of the Serene Prince, the members of
this restricted assembly agreed on a text stipulating that, according to the express will of Her Majesty, the tsarevich Peter Alexeyevich, still a minor and promised in marriage to Miss Maria
Menshikov, would, at the proper time, succeed the Empress Catherine I and would be assisted, until he came of age, by the Supreme Privy Council instituted by her. If he should die without
posterity, the document specified, the crown would redound to

his aunt Anna Petrovna and to her heirs; then to his other aunt, Elizabeth Petrovna, and to any heirs she might have. The two aunts would be members of the aforementioned Supreme Privy Council until the day their imperial nephew reached the age of 17. The formula conceived by Menshikov would give him the upper hand, through his daughter, the future tsarina, in managing the country's destiny.

This indirect confiscation of power galled Tolstoy and his usual collaborators, including Buturlin and the Portuguese adventurer Devier. They tried to respond, but Menshikov foiled their maneuver and counteracted by accusing them of the crime of lese-majesty. His paid spies gave him a positive report: the majority of Tolstoy's buddies were engaged in the plot. Under torture, the Portuguese Devier admitted to everything he was asked (the torturer must have handled the knout with considerable dexterity). He and his accomplices had publicly scorned the grief of Her Majesty' daughters and had participated in clandestine meetings with the intention of upsetting the monarchical order. In the name of the failing Empress, Menshikov had Tolstoy arrested; he was shut up in the Solovetsky Monastery, on an island in the White Sea; Devier was dispatched to Siberia; as for the others, they were simply sent back to their lands and told to stay there. Duke Charles Frederick of Holstein was not officially charged but, out of prudence and pride, he and his wife Anna, so wrongfully swindled, removed to their estate at Yekaterinhof.

The young couple had hardly left the capital when they were recalled: the tsarina had taken a turn for the worse. Decency and tradition required that her daughters attend her. Both came at a run to witness her final moments. After long suffering, she died on May 6, 1727, between 9:00 and 10:00 in the evening. At Menshikov's orders, two regiments of the Guard immediately encircled the Winter Palace to prevent any hostile demonstration. But nobody thought of protesting. Nor of crying, for that matter. Catherine's reign, which had lasted only two years and two months, left the majority of her subjects indifferent or perplexed. Should one regret or be pleased at her demise?

On May 8, 1727, Grand Duke Peter Alexeyevich was proclaimed emperor. The Secretary of the imperial cabinet, Makarov, announced the event to the courtiers and the dignitaries assembled at the palace. The terms of the proclamation, concocted with diabolic skill under Menshikov's leadership, linked the concept of choosing the sovereign (instituted by Peter the Great) with that of heredity, in conformity with the Muscovite tradition. "According to the will of Her Majesty, the late Empress," Makarov read in a solemn voice, "a new emperor has been *chosen*, in the person of an *heir*[6] to the throne: His Highness the Grand Duke Peter Alexeyevich." Listening to this proclamation, Menshikov exulted internally. His success was a miracle. Not only was his daughter virtually empress of Russia, but the Supreme Privy Council, which would exercise the role of regent until the majority of Peter II (who was as yet just 12 years old), was still entirely in his hands, as Serene Prince. That left him a good five years to bring the country to heel. He had no adversaries anymore; only subjects. Apparently, it was no longer necessary to be a Romanov in order to rule.

Ready to make any necessary compromise with the new power, Duke Charles Frederick of Holstein promised to keep quiet provided that, the moment Peter II reached the fateful age of 17, Anna and Elizabeth would receive two million rubles to be divided, as compensation. Moreover, Menshikov, who was having a good day, assured him that he would make every effort to support Charles Frederick's claims, as he was still stuck on the idea of retrieving his hereditary lands and would even like — why not? — to exercise his rights to the crown of Sweden. It was clear, now, to the Duke of Holstein, that his presence in St. Petersburg was only a step on the road toward the conquest of Stockholm — as though, in his eyes, the throne of the late King Charles XII was more prestigious than that of the one who had defeated him, the late Peter the Great.

This raging ambition was no surprise to Menshikov. Wasn't it due to a similar eagerness that he himself had arrived at a position that had been beyond his dreams back when he was only one of the tsar's companions in battles, banquets and beds? Where would he stop, in his rise to honors and fortune? At the moment when his future son-in-law was being proclaimed sovereign autocrat of all the Russias, under the name of Peter II, he began to think that his own reign might perhaps be just beginning.

Footnotes

1. Cited in Waliszewski: *L'Héritage de Pierre le Grand* [The Heritage of Peter the Great].
2. Hermann: *Geschichte des Russichen Staats*, quoted by Waliszewski, *op. cit.*
3. The duke of Bourbon succeeded Duke Philippe of Orleans as Regent, after the latter's death in 1723.
4. Reported by Hermann, *op. cit.*, and quoted by Waliszewski *op. cit.*
5. Remarks quoted by Daria Olivier: *Elizabeth I, Impératrice de Russie.*
6. Author's emphasis.

III

MACHINATIONS AROUND THE THRONE

Among all those who could have laid claim to the throne, the one who was least well-prepared for this frightening honor was the one who had just been given it. None of the candidates to succeed Catherine I had had a childhood so bereft of affection and guidance as the new tsar, Peter II. He never knew his mother, Charlotte of Brunswick-Wolfenbüttel, who died bringing him into the world, and he was only three years old when his father, the Tsarevich Alexis, succumbed under torture. Doubly orphaned, he was raised by governesses who were nothing but vulgar maidservants in the palace and by German and Hungarian tutors of little knowledge and little heart. He soon turned inward and exhibited, as soon as he reached the age of reason, a proud, aggressive and cynical nature. Always inclined to find fault and to rebel, the only person for whom he felt any tenderness was his sister Natalya, who was fourteen months older than he; he appreciated her vivacious temperament.

Out of atavism, no doubt, and in spite of his youth, he liked to get drunk and enjoyed the basest of jokes; he was astonished that the young lady enjoyed reading, serious conversations and studying foreign languages. She spoke German and French as fluently as Russian. What was she doing with all that twaddle? Wasn't it the role of a woman, by the age of 15 or 16, to enjoy herself, entertain others and seduce every worthy man who passes by? Peter teased her about her excessive application and she tried to discipline him by cajoling him with a softness to which he was not accustomed. What a pity that she was not prettier! But maybe it was better that way? What lessons might he not have given in to if, in addition to her sparkling spirit, she had had a desirable physique? Just as she was, she helped him to bear with his situation as a false sovereign whom everyone honored and whom nobody obeyed. Since his advent, Menshikov had relegated him to the rank of imperial figurehead. True, to mark his supremacy, he had arranged that at state dinners Menshikov should be seated to his left, whereas Natalya was to his right; and certainly, it was he who, installed upon a throne between his two aunts, Anna and Elizabeth, chaired the meetings of the Supreme Privy Council; true, he was soon to marry Menshikov's daughter, and Menshikov, once he became his father-in-law, would no doubt hand over the reins of power. But at present the young Peter was aware that he was only the shadow of an emperor, a caricature of Peter the Great, a masquerade-Majesty subjected to the will of the producer of the brilliant Russian spectacle. No matter what he was doing, Peter had to give in to the wishes of Menshikov, who had foreseen all and arranged all in his own way.

This omnipotent character had a palace located in the heart of St. Petersburg, situated in a superb park on Vasilievsky Island. While he waited for a bridge to be constructed for his personal use, Menshikov crossed the Neva in a rowing galley, the interior of which was hung with green velvet. Disembarking on the opposite bank, he would ride in a carriage with a gilded cab, emblazoned on the doors and the pediment with a princely crown. This masterpiece of craftsmanship and comfort, this heavenly chariot, was drawn by six horses harnessed in purple velvet, embroidered in gold and silver. Many heralds preceded Menshikov's every move about town. Two pages on horseback followed, two gentlemen of the court bounced along at the carriage doors, and six dragoons closed the parade and chased away the curious.[1] Nobody else in the capital surrounded his activities with such magnificence.

Peter suffered in silence from this ostentation that was putting the true tsar more in the shade with every passing day, so that even the people apparently no longer thought of him. To cap it all off, Menshikov waited until the emperor had taken his oath before the Guard to announce that, from now on, as a security measure, His Majesty would reside not at the Winter Palace but in his own palace, on Vasilievsky Island. Everyone was stunned to see the tsar thus placed "under the bell," but no one spoke up to protest. The principal opponents, Tolstoy, Devier and Golovkin, already had been exiled by the new master of Russia.

Having installed Peter — superbly, it is true — in his own residence, Menshikov kept close watch over the company he kept. The barricades that he placed at the doors of the imperial apartments were insuperable. Only the tsar's aunts, Anna and Elizabeth, his sister Natalya and a few trusted friends were allowed to visit him. Among the latter were the vice-chancellor Andrei Ivanovich Ostermann, the engineer and general Burkhard Christoph von Münnich (master of so many great works), Count Reinhold Loewenwolde (a former lover of Catherine I and paid agent of the duchess of Courland), the Scottish General Lascy (who was working for Russia and managed to stay out of trouble during the disorder that came on the heels of the empress's death), and finally and inevitably, the incorrigible Duke Charles Frederick of

Holstein, still haunted by the idea of returning Schleswig to the family holdings. Menshikov had indoctrinated them, and bribed them to prepare his future son-in-law to be an emperor only in name and to give up the conduct of affairs to him, definitively. Entrusting to them the education of this unreasonable and impulsive teenager, all he asked of them was to engender in him a taste for appearances rather than a taste for actions. For Menshikov, the ideal son-in-law would be a paragon of nullity and good manners. What did it matter if he were an ignoramus, if he had no concept of politics, as long as he knew how to conduct himself in the salon? Orders were given to His Majesty's entourage to keep him informed on matters superficially, but absolutely not in-depth. However, while the majority of the mentors chosen by Menshikov acceded to this instruction, the most cunning and most wily among the group had already begun to throw a wrench into the works.

Menshikov thought he had won the day; but meanwhile, the Westphalian Ostermann was gathering around him those who were most aggravated by the new dictator's vanity and arrogance. For a long time, they had observed Peter's mute hostility towards his virtual father-in-law, and they secretly supported their sovereign's cause. They were soon joined in their conspiracy by Peter's sister Natalya and by the two aunts, Anna and Elizabeth. When the instigators of this little tribal conspiracy urged him to join them, Duke Charles Frederick of Holstein also acknowledged that he would fight for the emancipation of Peter II, especially if that might be accompanied by a recognition of his own rights to Schleswig and — of course — to Sweden. Coincidentally, Elizabeth had just become engaged to another descendant of Holstein, Charles Augustus, first cousin of Charles Frederick, a candidate for the throne of Courland and bishop of Lübeck. This circumstance could only reinforce the Holstein clan's determination to shake off the yoke of Menshikov and to liberate Peter II from a humiliating guardianship.

Alas! June 1, 1727, the young bishop Charles Augustus was carried off by smallpox. Overnight, Elizabeth found herself with no suitor, no more marital hopes. After Louis XV balked, she now had lost another pretender — less prestigious, certainly, than the King of France, but a very honorable match for a Russian grand duchess. Really, fate seemed dead set against her dreams of marriage. She lost heart, took a strong dislike to the court of St. Petersburg and withdrew, with her putative brother-in-law Charles Frederick and her sister Anna, to the palace of Ekaterinhof, at the edge of St. Petersburg, under the shade trees of an immense park surrounded by canals. In this idyllic setting, she relied very much upon the affection of her close relations to help her ease her disappointment.

The very same day of their departure, Menshikov gave an extravagant feast at his palace in honor of the betrothal of his elder daughter, Maria, to the young Tsar Peter II. The intended, bedecked and bejeweled like a gilded coffer, received on this occasion the title of Her Most Serene Highness and the guarantee of an annual income of 34,000 rubles from the State Treasury. More parsimonious when it came to compensating the Tsarevna[2] Elizabeth, Menshikov only allocated 12,000 rubles to her to assuage the rigor of her mourning.[3] But Elizabeth wanted to be seen by one and all as an inconsolable fiancée. The fact that she was not yet married (by the age of 18), and that only the most ambitious seemed interested in her — and only out of political considerations — was too cruel a fate to be swallowed anytime soon. Fortunately, her friends immediately set about finding a high-quality substitute for Charles Augustus, in Russia or abroad. The dear departed's coffin had hardly been laid in the ground in Lübeck when the possible candidature of Charles Adolf of Holstein was suggested — the proper brother of the departed — and also that of Count Maurice of Saxony and several other gentlemen of easily verifiable merits.

While Elizabeth, at Ekaterinhof, was dreaming over these various parties, whose faces she barely recognized, in the heart of St. Petersburg Menshikov, as ever a practical man, was studying the available bachelors' relative advantages. In his eyes, the half-widowed tsarina represented an excellent bargaining chip in the diplomatic negotiations that were underway. But these matrimonial concerns did not make him lose sight of the education of his imperial pupil. Observing that Peter seemed to have become slightly less extravagant recently, he recommended to Ostermann that he step up his struggle against his pupil's natural idleness by accustoming him to fixed hours, whether they be spent in study or recreation. The Westphalian was assisted in this task by Prince Alexis Grigorievich Dolgoruky, the "assistant governor"; he often visited the palace with his young son, Prince Ivan, a beautiful, hot-blooded young man of 20 years, elegant and effeminate, who amused His Majesty with his inexhaustible chattering.

Upon her return from Ekaterinhof, where she had spent a few weeks in sentimental retirement, Elizabeth installed herself at the Summer Palace; but not a day went by that she did not pay a visit, with her sister Anna, to her dear nephew in his gilded cage. They would listen to the confidences of the spoiled child, share his passion for Ivan Dolgoruky — that irresistibly handsome young man — and keep them both company in their nightly revels. Despite the remonstrances of their male chaperons, a wind of madness blew through this shameless quartet. In December 1727, Johann Lefort brought the minister at the court of Saxony up to date on young Peter's escapades. "The master [Peter II] has no other occupation but to run in the streets, day and night, with the princess Elizabeth and her sister, to visit the chamberlain Ivan

[Dolgoruky], the pages, the cooks and God knows whom else."
Hinting that the sovereign under supervision had unnatural tastes
and that the delightful Ivan was inciting him in forbidden pleasures instead of curbing his inclinations, Lefort continued: "One
could almost believe that these misguided people [the Dolgoru-
kys] are encouraging the various vices by fostering [in the Tsar]
the sins of the Russia of the past. I know an apartment contigu-
ous to the billiard parlor where the deputy governor [Prince
Alexis Grigorievich Dolgoruky] hosts pleasure parties for him. . .
they don't go to bed until 7:00AM."[4]

That these young people should satiate their appetites in
such entertainment suited Menshikov just fine. As long as Peter
and his aunts continued to dope themselves in love intrigues and
casual affairs, their political influence would be nil. On the other
hand, the "Most Serene One" feared that Duke Charles Frederick
of Holstein, with his exasperating ambitions, might be ignoring
his wife Anna's warnings and might be overdoing things, in an
effort to destroy the *modus vivendi* that the Supreme Privy Council
had managed to impose upon the junior tsar and his close relatives. In order to cut short Charles Frederick's foolish dreams,
Menshikov took away from him (via an *ukase* that escaped Peter
II's vigilance one evening during a drunken binge) the island of
Oesel, in the Gulf of Riga, which the couple had received as a
wedding present, and cut back the duke's expense account. These
displays of pettiness were accompanied by so many minor vexa-
tions at the hand of Menshikov that the Duke and his wife were
annoyed for good and decided to leave the capital, where they
were treated like poor relations and intruders. Hugging her sister
before embarking with her husband for Kiel, with heart overflowing, Anna was gripped by a disastrous presentiment. She confided
to her friends that she was very much afraid of Menshikov's intrigues, on behalf of Elizabeth as well as Peter. She felt he was an

implacable enemy of their family. Because of his giant size and his broad shoulders, he was called the "proud Goliath," and Anna beseeched Heaven that Peter II, a new David, should bring down the monster of pride and spite that had such a hold on the empire.

After her sister departed for Holstein, Elizabeth tried at first to forget her sorrows and her fears in a swirl of romance and intrigue. Peter assisted her in this distracting enterprise by inventing new excuses for fooling around and intoxicating themselves every day. He was only 14 years old, yet he felt the desires of a man. To secure greater freedom of movement, Elizabeth and he emigrated to the old imperial palace of Peterhof. For a moment, they could believe that their secret vows were about to be fulfilled; for Menshikov, although he enjoyed an iron constitution, suddenly had a fainting spell and was spitting blood. He had to be confined to bed. According to the echoes that reached Peterhof, the doctors considered that the indisposition could be long lasting, if not fatal.

During this vacuum of power, the usual advisers met to comment on current matters. In addition to the illness of His Most Serene, another event of importance occurred meanwhile, and an embarrassing one, at that. Peter the Great's first wife, the Tsarina Eudoxia, whom he had imprisoned in the convent at Suzdal and then transferred to the fortress at Schlüsselburg, had suddenly resurfaced. The emperor had repudiated her in order to marry Catherine. An old woman, weak but still valiant after thirty years of reclusion, Eudoxia was the mother of the Tsarevich Alexis who had died under torture and the grandmother of Tsar Peter II who, by the way, had never met her and did not see any need to do so. Now that she was out of prison and Menshikov, her sworn enemy, was tied to his bed, the other members of the Supreme Privy Council thought that the grandson of this martyr, so worthy in her effacement, should pay her a visit of homage. They considered that to be even more advisable since the people saw Eudoxia as a saint who had been sacrificed for reasons of State. There was only one hitch, but it was a sizeable one: wouldn't Menshikov be furious if they took such an initiative without consulting him? Specialists in public issues discussed the matter gravely. Some suggested taking advantage of the young tsar's upcoming coronation, scheduled to take place in Moscow early in 1728, to set up a historic meeting between the grandmother (embodying the past) and the new tsar (embodying the future). Ostermann, Dolgoruky and other characters of lesser stature were already addressing messages of devotion to the old tsarina and requesting her support in future negotiations. But Eudoxia, immured in her prayers, fasting and memories, ignored the courtiers' agitation. She had suffered too much already from the contaminated atmosphere of the palaces to wish for any other reward than peace in the light of the Lord.

While the grandmother was aspiring to eternal rest, the grandson, his head on fire, was spinning out of control. But it was not the illusion of grandeur that haunted him. Worlds away from the legendary *babushka*, Elizabeth was leading him from one party to another. Hunting meets alternated with impromptu picnics, with a roll in the hay at some rustic cottage, with reveries in the moonlight. A light perfume of incest spiced the pleasure Peter took in caressing his young aunt. There's nothing like guilt to save lovemaking from the tedium of habit. If you play by the rules, relations between a man and a woman quickly become as tiresome as doing one's duty. That conviction must have been what encouraged Peter to throw himself into parallel experiments with Ivan Dolgoruky. In thanks for the intimate satisfactions that Ivan gave him, Peter — with the approval of Elizabeth — named him chamberlain and awarded him the Order of St. Catherine, which was reserved, theoretically, for ladies.

The people at court were outraged and the foreign diplomats were quick to comment, in their dispatches, on His Majesty's two-way escapades. They were already prepared to bury His Most Serene. Little did they suspect how great was Menshikov's physical resistance. Suddenly, he popped up again in the midst of this circus of ambitious and sexual maneuvering. Did he think he could just raise his voice, and the troublemakers would run for shelter? Hardly. By now, Peter II had gotten the upper hand. He would no longer tolerate anyone, including his future father-in-law, thwarting his desires. In front of Menshikov — stunned and close to apoplexy — he howled, "I will show you who is master, here!"[5]

This outburst reminded Menshikov of the terrible rages of his former master, Peter the Great. Understanding that it would be imprudent to defy a lamb that had gone mad, he pretended to see this fury as nothing but a late childish tantrum, and departed Peterhof, where Peter had received him so badly, to convalesce at his property at Oranienbaum. Before leaving, he took care to invite all the assembled company to a reception that he was planning to host in his country residence in honor of the tsar and to celebrate his own recovery. But Peter II persisted and, under the pretext that His Most Serene did not invite Elizabeth by name, refused to attend. To underscore his displeasure, he openly went out with his aunt to hunt big game in the surroundings.

Throughout this semi-hunting, semi-romantic escapade, he wondered what was going on at the celebrations dreamed up by Menshikov. Wasn't it strange that none of his friends had followed his example? Was their fear of displeasing Menshikov so strong that they preferred to displease the tsar? In any case, he didn't worry much about the feelings of Maria Menshikov, who seemed to have gone from intended-bride to back-on-the-shelf. On the contrary, as soon as Menshikov's guests were back from

Oranienbaum, he questioned them avidly on how the Serene One had seemed during the festivities. Pressed to speak their minds, they told him everything, in detail. They insisted, in particular, on the fact that Menshikov had pushed his insolence to the point of sitting, in their presence, on the throne prepared for Peter II. To hear them tell it, their host, consumed with pride, conducted himself in every way as though he were the master of the empire. Ostermann declared that he was offended as much as if it had been him that the Serene One had slighted. The next day, taking advantage of an absence of Peter II, who had gone out hunting with Elizabeth, Ostermann received Menshikov at Peterhof and reproached him, in a dry tone, in the name of all the sincere friends of the imperial family, for his unseemly conduct towards His Majesty. Piqued by these remonstrances from a subordinate, Menshikov took umbrage and returned to St. Petersburg, contemplating a revenge that would forever remove the desire to plot against him from this scheming band.

Arriving at his palace on Vasilievsky Island, he was stunned to see that all of Peter II's furniture had been removed and transported to the Summer Palace (Peterhof) where the tsar, he was informed, intended to reside from now on. Outraged, the Most Serene Prince rushed to the headquarters of the Guard to demand an explanation from the officers charged with keeping watch over the tsar. All the sentinels had already been relieved and the station chief announced, with an air of contrition, that he was only following imperial orders. Apparently, there was another hand pulling the strings. What might have looked, at first, like the whim of a prince seemed, in fact, to signal a final breakdown. For Menshikov, this was the collapse of an edifice that he had been building for years and that he had believed to be as solid as the granite of the quays along the Neva.

What a catastrophe! Who was behind it? There could be no

doubt. Alexis Dolgoruky and his son, the ravishing and under-handed Ivan, must have masterminded it all. How could Menshi-kov save whatever might still be salvageable? Should he beg for leniency from those who had cut him down, or turn to Peter and try to plead his cause directly? Even as he pondered these unpal-atable options, he heard that the tsar, having joined his aunt Elizabeth at the Summer Palace, had convened the members of the Supreme Privy Council and that he was discussing with them what additional sanctions should be taken. The verdict came down before the defendant could even prepare his defense. Most probably egged on by Elizabeth, Natalya and the Dolgoruky clan, Peter ordered the Serene One arrested. When Major General Simon Saltykov came to inform him of his condemnation, Menshi-kov could only write a letter of protest and justification, which he doubted would ever be transmitted to the intended recipient.

The next day the charges began to mount, increasingly iniq-uitous, increasingly defamatory. Stripped of his titles and privi-leges, Menshikov was exiled to his own estate, for life — in other words, he was permanently grounded. With whatever posses-sions he could throw together on the spot, the condemned left St. Petersburg by slow caravan — and no one came out to see him off. He who had been everything, yesterday, was a nonentity today. His most enthusiastically obliged friends became his worst ene-mies. And the tsar's hatred continued unabated. At every stage along the road, a missive from the palace announced a new dis-grace for him. At Vyshny-Volochok came an order to disarm the deposed favorite's servants; at Tver, it was announced that he had taken too many servants, horses and carriages — those in excess were to be returned to St. Petersburg; at Klin came the order to confiscate from Miss Maria Menshikov, ex-fiancée of the tsar, the ring by which he had pledged his troth; and finally, at the ap-proaches to Moscow, came an order to by-pass the old city of kings and to continue without delay to Orenburg, in the remote province of Riazan.[6]

Reaching that city at the border between European Russia and Western Siberia, on November 3, Menshikov, his heart in his throat, got his first view of the place to which he had been relegated. The house, enclosed behind the crenellated walls of a fortress, looked perfectly suited to serve as a prison. Sentinels were assembled to guard every exit. An officer was charged with surveillance over the family's comings and goings. All of Menshikov's correspondence was inspected before being forwarded. Menshikov refused to admit defeat; he tried to redeem himself by sending messages of repentance to those who had condemned him.

However, at roughly the same time, the Supreme Privy Council received a report from Count Nicholas Golovin, Russia's ambassador in Stockholm. This confidential document denounced some of the Serene Prince's recent intrigues. Prior to his dismissal, he apparently had picked up some 5,000 ducats from the English for informing Sweden of the dangers posed by Russia's support for the Duke of Holstein's territorial claims. This treason by a Russian dignitary to the benefit of a foreign power opened the way with a new series of denouncements and heavy blows. Hundreds of letters, some signed, some anonymous, piled up on the table at the Supreme Privy Council. Emulating each other, ganging up on someone who was down, everyone reproached Menshikov for his suspicious sources of income and for the millions of gold coins discovered in his various houses. Johann Lefort even thought it useful to let his government know that the silver vessel seized on December 20 in a secret cache at Menshikov's principal residence weighed 70 poods[7] and that they hoped to find additional treasures during subsequent searches. The accumulated evidence of abuse of power, embezzlement, theft and treason merited that the Supreme Privy Council sanction him mercilessly. The initial punishment was considered to have been too soft; a legal commission was established to handle the matter. The commission began by arresting the unmasked despot's three secretaries. Then Menshikov was given a twenty-point questionnaire, and ordered to respond "as soon as possible."

However, whereas they had agreed on the need for eliminating Menshikov, the members of the Supreme Privy Council were bickering among themselves as to how to distribute the power after his downfall. Ostermann had initially taken charge of current affairs; but the Dolgorukys, on the strength of their family's seniority, became increasingly impatient to supplant "the Westphalian." Their direct rivals were the Golitsyns, whose family tree was, according to them, at least equally glorious. Each party was grasping for as much as it could get, without overly concerning themselves about Peter II nor Russia. Since the tsar's only preoccupation was to have fun, there was no reason for the great servants of the State to tax themselves overmuch in defending the welfare and the prosperity of the country instead of looking to their own interests. The Dolgorukys counted on young Ivan, so attractive and seductive, to turn the tsar against his aunt Elizabeth and her sister Natalya, whose ambitions seemed suspicious. For his part, Dmitri Golitsyn charged his son-in-law, the elegant and none too scrupulous Alexander Buturlin, with engaging His Majesty in varied enough pleasures to keep his mind off politics. But Elizabeth and Natalya suspected what the Dolgorukys and Golitsyns were up to. Together, they tried to open the young tsar's eyes, alerting him to the dangers that lurked behind those pleasant smiles with the sharp teeth.

However, Peter had inherited his ancestors' inability to tolerate any restraint, and he took every argument as an insult to his dignity. He rebuffed his sister and his aunt. Natalya did not insist; as for Elizabeth, she went over to the enemy. As a consequence of spending so much time with her nephew's friends, she fell in love with the very same Alexander Buturlin that she had intended to combat. Giving in to the unrestrained license of her nephew, she readily joined him in every manifestation of frivolity. Hunting and lovemaking became, for her as well as for him, the two poles of their activity. And who better than Buturlin could satisfy their common taste for the unpredictable and the provocative? Of course, the Supreme Privy Council and, through it, all the court and all the embassies, were kept abreast of the tsar's extravagances. They began to think it was high time to give him the crown and make him settle down. It was in this atmosphere of libertinage and infighting that the political leaders of Russia prepared the coronation ceremonies in Moscow.

On January 9, 1728, Peter set out at the head of a procession as grand as one can imagine for such an exodus, with all of St. Petersburg in his wake. Through the cold and the snow, the nobility and the high officials of the new capital slowly headed off for the pomp and celebrations at the old Kremlin. But in Tver, halfway to Moscow, the tsar was taken ill. It was feared that he might have measles; the doctors recommended at least two weeks' bed rest. Only on February 4 did the young sovereign, finally recovered, make his solemn entry into a Moscow bedecked in flags and bunting, overflowing with cheers and thundering with cannon blasts and the ringing of bells. His first stop, according to protocol, was to pay a visit his grandmother, the empress Eudoxia. He felt no emotion toward this old woman, tired and driveling, and he was even irritated when she reproached him for his dissolute life and recommended he marry as soon as possible a wise and wellborn girl. Cutting short the interview, he curtly sent her back to her prayers and her good works. This reaction did not surprise the wife repudiated by Peter the Great. It was clear to her that the teenager had inherited his grandfather's independence of mind, cynicism and cruelty. But his genius? She feared not!

It was the Dolgorukys who organized the ceremonies. The date of February 24, 1728 was selected for the coronation of the tsar, in the heart of the Kremlin, in the Cathedral of the Assumption. Tucked away in a latticework booth at the back of the church, the tsarina Eudoxia watched her grandson don the crown and take in one hand the scepter and in the other the sphere, complementary symbols of power. Blessed by a priest who seemed to have stepped right out of one of the icons, in his double-gilded and embroidered chasuble, lofted to the high heavens by the singing of the choir, wreathed in clouds of incense, the tsar waited for the end of the liturgy and, as he had been told to do, went up to his grandmother and kissed her hand. He promised her that he would see to it that she would be surrounded by all the chamberlains, pages and ladies-in-waiting that her high rank deserved, even if, as seemed desirable, she should choose to settle somewhere outside the capital to avoid the agitation of the court. Eudoxia got the message, and she removed to another residence. Everyone in Peter's retinue heaved a sigh of relief: no major incident had occurred to mar the festivities.

However, a few days after the coronation, the police at the Kremlin gates discovered some anonymous letters denouncing the Dolgorukys' turpitude and inviting people of good heart to demand the rehabilitation of Menshikov. Public rumor attributed these letters to the Golitsyn family, whose animosity towards the Dolgorukys was well-known. But the Supreme Privy Council, not having any proof to give to the board of inquiry and following the lead of the Dolgorukys, decided that Menshikov alone must be behind this call to rebellion; they ordered that he and his family be exiled to Berezov, deep in Siberia. Just when the former court favorite thought he was done with the tsar's justice, two officers presented themselves at his house of Orenburg, within the fortress, read him the sentence and, without giving him time to turn around, shoved him into a carriage. His terrified wife and children climbed in beside him. They were all preemptively dispossessed, and were left with only some farm animals and a bit of furniture, out of charity. The convoy straggled along the route, escorted by a detachment of soldiers — with weapons drawn, as if they were transferring a dangerous criminal.

Berezov, located more than a thousand versts (675 miles) from Tobolsk, is a godforsaken hole in the middle of a wasteland of tundra, forests and marshes. The winter is so severe there that the cold, they say, kills birds in full flight and shatters the windowpanes of the houses. Such misery, after so much wealth and honor, was not enough to undermine Menshikov's fortitude. His wife, Daria, died of exhaustion along the way. His daughters wept over their lost dreams of love and grandeur, forever gone, and he himself regretted having lived through so much woe. However, an irrepressible instinct of self-preservation impelled him to keep his head during this adversity. Accustomed as he was to preening in palaces, he labored with his hands, as a simple workman, to put together an *izba* for himself and his family. The neighbors, informed of his "crimes" against the emperor, shunned him and even threatened him with violence. One day a hostile crowd gathered, shouting insults and throwing stones at him and his daughters in the street; he shouted back, "If you're going to throw stones, only throw them at me! Spare the women!"[8] Nevertheless, after a few months of these daily affronts, he did begin to deteriorate; finally, he gave up the fight. An attack of apoplexy carried off the colossus in November 1729. One month later, his elder daughter Maria, the tsar's little fiancée, followed him to the grave.[9]

Indifferent to the fate of those whose demise he had precipitated, Peter II went his merry way, continuing his pleasure-filled and chaotic existence. Not having to account to him for any of their decisions, the Dolgorukys, Golitsyns and the clever Ostermann utilized the opportunity to impose their will at every occasion. However, they were still wary of Elizabeth's influence over her nephew. She alone, they believed, might be able to neutralize the power that the darling Ivan Dolgoruky was gaining over His Majesty, which was so essential to their cause. The best means of disarming her, obviously, would be to marry her off at once. But to whom? Thoughts turned once again to Count Maurice of Saxony. But Elizabeth didn't care a fig about him. Her charming cranium held no thoughts beyond the next romp. Sure of her power over men, she threw herself at one after another for casual idylls and liaisons. After seducing Alexander Buturlin, she went after Ivan Dolgoruky, the Tsar's designated "sweetie." Was she excited by the idea of charming a partner whose homosexual preferences were well-known? Her sister, Anna Petrovna, retired in Holstein, had just brought a son[10] into the world, whereas Elizabeth, at the age of 19, was still unmarried; she was far more concerned, however, with weaving her nefarious intrigue with the darling Ivan. She was stimulated by the adventure, as if she were trying to prove the superiority of her sex in all forms of perversity in love. Probably she thought it less banal, and thus more interesting, to take a man from another man than to steal him from a woman.

During the festivities held in Kiel by Anna Petrovna and the Grand Duke Charles Frederick to celebrate the birth of their child, the tsar opened the ball with Elizabeth. After dancing with her gallantly, under the charmed gaze of the assembly, he withdrew to the next room, according to his custom, with his drinking buddies. Having knocked back a few glasses, he noted that Ivan, his usual companion at such events, was not at his side. Surprised, he walked back and saw him dancing, breathlessly, in the middle of the ballroom with Elizabeth. She looked so excited, face to face with this cavalier who was devouring her with his eyes, that Peter lost his temper and went back to get drunk. But which one was he really jealous over? Ivan or Elizabeth?

Aunt and nephew were only reconciled after Easter. Forsaking Dolgoruky for once, Peter took Elizabeth along on an extended shooting party. The expedition was expected to last several months. A 500-person retinue accompanied the couple. Wild fowl as well as large game were the quarries. When the time came to track a wolf, a fox or a bear, valets in silver-trimmed green livery did the job. They would attack the animal with rifles and spears, under the interested eyes of the Masters. After a perusal of the hunting spectacle, a banquet would be held in the open air, followed by a visit to the merchants who came from far and wide to display their fabrics, embroideries, miraculous ointments and costume jewelry.

A piece of alarming news caught Peter and Elizabeth by surprise in the midst of all this revelry: Natalya, Peter's sister, took sick; she was spitting blood. Was she going to die? But no, she recovered; instead, Elizabeth's sister in Kiel, Anna Petrovna, Duchess of Holstein, gave her close relatives more serious concern. She had caught cold while watching the fireworks during her churching. Pneumonia, the doctors declared; and in a few days, she was gone. The poor thing was only 20 years old; and she left an orphaned son, Charles Ulrich, just two weeks old. Everyone around Peter was dismayed. He alone expressed no regret at her passing. Some wondered whether he was still capable of human feeling. Was it the excessive indulgence in forbidden pleasures that had desiccated his heart?

When the body of his aunt, of whom he used to be so fond, was brought back to St. Petersburg, he didn't bother to go to the burial. And he didn't even cancel the ball that was habitually given at the palace at that time. A few months later, in November

1728, it was his sister Natalya's turn — her consumption, which had been thought to be under control, abruptly took a turn for the worse. Although Peter was, as it happened, off hunting and fooling around in the countryside, he resigned himself to a return to St. Petersburg in order to be at the patient's bedside for her final moments. He impatiently listened to Ostermann's and Natalya's friends lamentations, and their praise of the virtues of this princess "who was an angel." As soon as she died, December 3, 1728, he rushed off again for the domain of Gorenky, where the Dolgorukys were preparing another of their formidable shooting parties for him. This time, he did invite Elizabeth to accompany him. Without exactly being tired of the young woman's attentions and coquetry, he felt the need for a change in personnel among his playmates. To justify his fickleness, people said that it was normal for a healthy man to enjoy a succession of relationships more than dreary fidelity.

At the palace, at Gorenky, a happy surprise awaited him. Alexis, the head of the Dolgoruky clan and a skilful organizer of hunts for his guest, introduced Peter to a new breed of game: the prince's three daughters, all fresh, available and tempting, with an air of provocative virginity. The eldest, Catherine (Katya to close friends), was breathtakingly beautiful, with ebony hair, eyes of black flame and a soft, matte skin that flushed pink with the least emotion. Bold of temperament, she was a full participant in everything from stag hunt to banquet and toasts; she was clever at parlor games and graceful at the impromptu dances that were put on after hours of riding through the countryside. Observers agreed in predicting that Ivan would soon be supplanted by his sister, the delightful Katya, in the heart of the inconstant tsar. Either way, the Dolgoruky family was ahead.

However, in St. Petersburg, the rivals of the Dolgoruky coalition feared that this passing fancy, the reverberations of which were already being heard, might lead to marriage. Such a union would end up making the tsar totally subservient to his in-laws and would close the door on the other members of the Supreme Privy Council. Peter seemed to be so smitten by his Katya that he had hardly returned to St. Petersburg when he decided to leave again. If he bothered to stop in the capital at all, it was only to round out his hunting gear. Having bought 200 hunting hounds and 400 greyhounds, he headed back to Gorenky. But, back where he'd enjoyed such great exploits in the field, he no longer seemed very sure how much fun he was having. He was bored, counting the hares, foxes and wolves that he had killed in the course of the day. One evening, citing the three bears listed in his hunting record, somebody complimented him for this latest prowess. With a sarcastic smile, he replied: "I did better than take three bears; I'm taking with me four two-footed animals." His interlocutor recognized that as an unkind allusion to prince Alexis Dolgoruky and his three daughters. Such mockery, in public, made people suppose that, after the initial combustion, perhaps the tsar no longer burned so intensely for Katya and that he might be on the verge of abandoning her.

Ostermann, an astute strategist, followed the ups and downs of this unpredictable couple from afar, through the gossip and rumor mills of the court. Now he set about preparing a counteroffensive. Her grief at the death of her sister Anna having run its course, Elizabeth was again available. Admittedly, her thoughts often turned toward that baby, her nephew, deprived of tenderness and growing up at a distance, practically becoming a stranger. She wondered, from time to time, whether she should not draw him back in, nearer to her. And then the events of the day would distract her from these thoughts, so worthy of a guardian. It was even said that after a mystical crisis, she was experiencing such a new zest for life that she had fallen under the spell of the charming heir of a great family, the very seductive Count Simon Naryshkin. This magnificent and refined gentleman was of the same age as she, and his assiduous pursuit, over hill and dale, like an indefatigable barbet spaniel, showed how much they both enjoyed their tête-à-têtes. When she withdrew to her estate at Ismailovo, she invited him over. There, they enjoyed the healthy and simple joys of the countryside. What could be pleasanter than playing in the country with palaces and flocks of servants in the background? Every day they went to collect nuts, pick flowers, and hunt for mushrooms, speaking with a paternal kindness to the serfs on the estate, taking an interest in the health of the animals grazing in the meadows or ruminating in the cattle sheds. While Ostermann quizzed the spies whom he had sent to Ismailovo, keeping tabs on the progress of Simon Naryshkin and Elizabeth's bucolic love affair, the Dolgorukys in Gorenky continued to cherish, in spite of some alarms, the idea of a marriage between Katya and the tsar.

To cover all the bases, they thought it would be appropriate not only to wed Tsar Peter II to Catherine Dolgoruky, but for good measure to marry his aunt Elizabeth to Ivan Dolgoruky, as well. However, now the latest tidings held that the idiotic Elizabeth was infatuated with Naryshkin. Such an unexpected crush was liable to upset the entire plan. This would have to be stamped out at once! Going for broke, the Dolgorukys threatened to have Elizabeth locked up in a convent for misconduct if she insisted on preferring Naryshkin over Dolgoruky. But the young woman had the blood of Peter the Great in her veins, and in a flash of pride, she refused to obey. The Dolgorukys, however, had all the connections. The principal apparatuses of the State did their bidding, and Naryshkin received an order from the Supreme Privy Council to set out immediately on a foreign mission. He would be kept abroad for as long as necessary for Elizabeth to forget about him.

Frustrated once more in love, she wept, raged and pondered how to take her revenge. However, she quickly recognized that she was impotent to fight against the machinations of the High Council. And she could not even count on Peter to defend her interests anymore: he was far too absorbed by his own sentimental problems to deal with those of his aunt. According to the gossip, he had almost repudiated Katya when he learned that she had had clandestine meetings with another aspirant, a certain Count Millesimo, an attaché at the German embassy in Russia. Frightened by the consequences of such a break-up, and under pressure to keep the tsar from balking, the Dolgorukys arranged for a discreet tête-à-tête between Katya and Peter, in a hunting lodge, hoping for a reconciliation. And that very evening, showing up just at the moment of the first caresses, the girl's father declared the family's honor to have been outraged and he demanded formal reparations. The strangest thing is that this crude subterfuge bore fruit. It is impossible to know whether the "culprit" thus surprised *in flagrante delicto* by an indignant *pater familias* finally gave in to his feelings for Katya, to fear of scandal, or simply to laziness.

In any event, on Catherine's birthday, October 22, 1729, the Dolgorukys revealed to their guests that the girl had just been promised in marriage to the Tsar. On November 19, the Supreme Privy Council received the official announcement of the engagement and, on the 30th, a religious ceremony was held in Moscow at Lefortovo Palace, where Peter generally stayed during his brief stops in that city. The old tsarina Eudoxia agreed to come out of retirement to bless the young couple. All the dignitaries of the empire, all the foreign ambassadors were present in the room, awaiting the arrival of the bride-elect. Her brother Ivan, Peter's former favorite, went to escort her from Golovin Palace, where she was staying with her mother. The procession traversed the city, cheered by a crowd of good people who, looking on such youth and such magnificence, thought they beheld the happy conclusion of a fairytale. At the entrance to the Lefortovo Palace, the crown surmounting the roof of the coach in which the bride was riding struck the lintel of the gateway and crashed resoundingly to the pavement. Superstitious onlookers saw this incident as a bad omen.

But Katya did not stumble. Crossing the threshold of the ceremonial hall, she stood perfectly straight. Bishop Feofan Prokopovich invited her to come forward with Peter. The couple took their places under a silver and gold canopy held aloft by two generals. After the rings were exchanged, artillery salutes and pealing bells preceded a long stream of congratulations. According to protocol, the Tsarevna Elizabeth Petrovna stepped forward and, trying to forget that she was the daughter of Peter the Great, kissed the hand of a "subject" named Catherine Dolgoruky. A bit later, it was Peter II's turn to swallow his spite, for the Count de Millesimo, having approached Catherine, was bowing down before her. She was just about to extend her hand to him. Peter would have liked to prevent that gesture of courtesy, which he considered out of place. But she moved too quickly, and spontaneously presented her fingers to the attaché, who brushed them with his lips before standing straight again, under the murderous gaze of the groom. Seeing the tsar's rage, Millesimo's friends took him by the elbow and propelled him into the crowd, where they disappeared. At this point Prince Vasily Dolgoruky, one of the most eminent members of this large family, felt that the proper time had come to address a short homily to his niece. "Yesterday, I was your uncle," he said, facing a circle of attentive listeners. "Now, you are my sovereign and I am your faithful servant. However, I call upon my former rights in giving you this advice: do not look upon the one whom you are marrying as your husband only, but also as your master, and make it your only concern to please him. . . . If any member of your family asks you for a favor, forget it and consider only the merits of the situation. That will be the best means of ensuring all the happiness that I wish you."[1]

These judicious words completely spoiled Peter's mood. He scowled until the end of the reception. Even during the fireworks at the end of the celebration, he did not so much as glance at the woman with whom he had just exchanged pledges of eternal love and confidence. The more he looked out at the faces surrounding him, the more he felt that he had fallen into a trap.

While he had allowed himself to be buffeted about between political intrigues, women, drink and the pleasures of hunting, the Supreme Privy Council had, after a fashion, managed the affairs of State. At the initiative of these wise men and with the tsar's concurrence, measures were taken to reinforce their control over the magistrature, to regulate the use of bills of exchange, to ban the clergy from wearing lay clothing and to keep knowledge of Russia's problems reserved to the Senate. In short, in spite of the emperor's defection, the empire went on.

Meanwhile, Peter learned that his sweetheart Ivan Dolgoruky was planning to marry little Natalya Sheremetiev. To be honest, he did not see much problem in giving up his former favorite to a rival. It was agreed that, to affirm the bond of friendship between the four young people, their two marriages should be celebrated the same day. However, this reasonable arrangement still troubled Peter. Everything and everybody had disappointed him and annoyed him. There was no place where he could feel comfortable and he did not have anyone whom he felt he could trust.

Shortly before the end of the year, he paid a surprise visit to Elizabeth, whom he had neglected for the last several months. He found her poorly housed, poorly served, and lacking the essentials — whereas she should have been the first lady in the empire. He had gone to her to complain about his own distress, and instead it was she who complained to him about her destitution. She accused the Dolgorukys of having humiliated her, of ruining her and of preparing to dominate him through the wife that they had tossed into his arms. Shaken by his aunt's complaints (and still secretly in love with her), he answered, "This is not my fault! No one obeys me; but I will soon find the means to break my chains!"[12]

These remarks were reported to the Dolgorukys, who put their heads together to work out a response that would be effective while preserving the appearance of respecting the tsar. Moreover, they had another family problem on their hands that required urgent intervention: Ivan had fallen out with his sister Katya, who had lost all sense of restraint since her engagement and was laying claim to the late Grand Duchess Natalya's diamonds, saying that the tsar had promised them to her. This sordid quarrel over a box of jewels was liable to irritate Peter just at the moment when they needed more than ever to dampen his mistrust. But how could they make a woman listen to reason, when she was less sensitive to male logic than to the glitter of precious stones?

On January 6, 1730, at the time of the traditional blessing of the waters of the Neva, Peter arrived late at the ceremony and positioned himself behind the open sledge in which Catherine was seated. In the frozen air, the chanting of the priest and the singing of the choir resonated weirdly; vapor rose from the mouths of the singers. Peter shivered throughout the interminable service. Returning home, he could not stop shaking; he was put to bed. They thought he'd gotten a chill. And anyway, by January 12, he had recovered. But, five days later, the doctors detected symptoms of small pox, which was often fatal at the time. Receiving this news, all the Dolgorukys gathered together at the Golovin palace in terror. They already foresaw the worst and started looking for ways to avert the catastrophe. Amid the general panic, Alexis Dolgoruky stated that only one solution existed, should the tsar die suddenly: to crown his chosen bride Catherine, little Katya, without delay. But this claim struck Prince Vasily Vladimirovich as exorbitant, and he protested in the name of all the family.

"Neither I nor any of mine will wish to be her subjects! She is not married!"

"She is promised in marriage!" retorted Alexis.

"That's not the same at all!"

A heated debate erupted. Prince Sergei Dolgoruky suggested raising the Guard to support the cause of the tsar's fiancée. Turning toward General Vasily Vladimirovich Dolgoruky, he exclaimed:

"You and Ivan control the Preobrazhensky regiment. Together, the two of you can make your men do whatever you want!"

"We would be massacred!" retorted the General; and he walked out of the meeting.

After he left, another Dolgoruky, Prince Vasily Lukich, a member of the Supreme Privy Council, sat down by the fireplace where an enormous wood fire as burning and, on his own authority, drafted a will for the tsar to sign — while he still had the strength to read and sign an official document. The other members of the family flocked around him and suggested a sentence here, a word there to refine the text. When he was done, someone in the group spoke up, voicing the fear that their adversaries would dispute the authenticity of the document. A third Dolgoruky, Ivan, Peter's little friend and the fiancé of Natalya Sheremetiev, came to the rescue. Did they need the tsar's signature? Aha! He pulled a piece of paper from his pocket and showed it to his relatives.

"Here is the tsar's handwriting," he said, cheerfully. "And

here is mine. You yourselves would not be able to tell them apart. And I know how to sign his name as well; I often did so as a joke!"

The onlookers were flabbergasted — but not indignant. Dipping a quill into the inkwell, Ivan signed Peter's name at the bottom of the page. They all leaned over his shoulder and murmured with wonder.

"That is exactly the hand of the tsar!"[13] they exclaimed.

Then the conspirators exchanged half-reassured glances and prayed God that they would be spared the necessity of actually using this forgery.

From time to time, they sent emissaries to the palace for an update on the tsar's condition. The news was grimmer and grimmer. Peter died at one o'clock in the morning, Monday, January 19, 1730, at the age of 14 years and three months. His reign had lasted just over two and a half years. January 19, 1730, the day of his death, is the date he had set a few weeks before for his marriage with Catherine Dolgoruky.

Footnotes

1. Cf. Brian-Chaninov: *Histoire de Russie*.
2. A traditional term designating the daughter of the tsar.
3. Cf. Daria Olivier, *op. cit.*
4. Cf. Waliszewski, *L'Héritage de Pierre le Grand.*
5. Cf. Daria Olivier, *op. cit.*
6. Details provided by Essipov: "L'Exil du prince Menshikov," *Annales de la Patrie, 1861,* and cited by Waliszewski, *op. cit.*
7. Almost 2500 lbs.
8. Waliszewski, *op. cit.*
9. Menshikov's two other children, his son Alexander and his daughter Alexandra, were recalled from exile only under the following reign.
10. The future Peter III, who would marry Catherine the Great.
11. Cited by Soloviov: *Histoire de Russie*, quoted by K Waliszewski, *op. cit.*
12. *Ibid.*
13. Details found in the State Archives (Moscow) file on the Dolgoruky scandal, and quoted by Kostomarov in his *Monograph* and by K. Waliszewski, *op. cit.*

IV

The Surprise Accession of Anna Ivanovna

The same uncertainty that had embarrassed the members of the Supreme Privy Council upon the death of Peter the Great gripped them again in the hours following the demise of Peter II. In the absence of a male heir and an authentic will, who could replace the late ruler without sparking a revolution among the aristocracy?

The usual notables were gathered at Lefortovo Palace in Moscow, with the Golitsyns, Golovkins and Dolgorukys at the center. But nobody had the nerve, at first, to voice an opinion — as if all the titled "decision-makers" felt guilty for the tragic decline of the monarchy. Taking advantage of the general confusion, Vasily Dolgoruky chose his moment and, hoisting his sword, gave a rallying cry: "Long live Her Majesty, Catherine!" And he cited the recently fabricated will, to justify this proclamation of victory. Thanks to this intrigue, the Dolgorukys had a chance of attaining the highest position in the empire. The goal was worth a little cheating. But the clan of those who opposed that choice struck back at once: Dmitri Golitsyn stared down Vasily Dolgoruky and sharply asserted that the will was false.

And he looked as though he could somehow prove it. The Dolgorukys, fearing that the document would not stand up to serious examination and that they would then be liable to serious charges of counterfeit, decided not to push their luck any further. That was the end of it for Catherine; there was no more talk of giving her a throne. Just as she was poised to take her seat, it was whisked out from under her. Pressing his advantage, Dmitri Golitsyn declared that in the absence of a male successor directly descended from Peter the Great, the Supreme Privy Council should turn to the offspring of the elder branch and offer the crown to one of the children of Peter I's brother Ivan V (known as "the Simple"; although sickly and indolent, he had been "co-tsar" with Peter the Great during the five years when their sister Sophia had served as regent).

But, as luck would have it, Ivan V had produced only female progeny. So that even in that case, they would have to accept a woman ruler for Russia. Wasn't that dangerous? Another harsh debate broke out over the advantages and disadvantages of a "gynocracy." Admittedly, Catherine I had recently proven that a woman can be courageous, determined and clear-minded when circumstances require. However, as everyone knows, "that sex" is slave to the senses. Thus a female sovereign would be likely to sacrifice the grandeur of the fatherland for the pleasures dispensed by her lover. Those who supported this thesis bolstered it by citing Menshikov who, they pointed out, had led Catherine by the nose. But wouldn't a tsar be as weak as the tsarina had been in the hands of the Most Serene, if he had a lover who was as adept and skilful at both loving and intrigues? Didn't Peter II himself demonstrate complete abdication of authority under the wiles of female seduction? So that what mattered, when it came to choosing whom to place on the throne, was not the gender *per se* so much as the character of the individual in whom the country was placing its confidence. Under these conditions, asserted Dmitri Golitsyn, a matriarchy would be entirely acceptable, provided that the individual being offered such an honor was worthy to assume it.

This principle having been accepted by everyone present, he went on to consider the remaining candidates. From the very beginning, he brushed aside the absurd idea of installing Elizabeth Petrovna, Peter II's aunt, since in his opinion she would have given up the succession implicitly by leaving the capital to live as a recluse in the countryside, bad-mouthing all her relatives and complaining about everything. All three daughters of Ivan V seemed more promising, to him, than this daughter of Peter the Great. However, the eldest, Catherine Ivanovna, was known for her strange moods and crotchety temperament. Moreover her husband, Prince Charles Leopold of Mecklenburg, was a nervous and unstable man, an eternal rebel, always ready to fight — be it against his neighbors or his subjects. The fact that Catherine Ivanovna had lived apart from him for ten years was not a sufficient guarantee for, if she were proclaimed empress, he would return to her at a gallop and would never stop dragging the country into costly and useless wars. The youngest, Praskovya Ivanovna, rickety and scrofulous, had neither the health, the clear thinking, nor the moral balance required to manage public affairs. That left the second, Anna Ivanovna. She admitted to being 37 years old, and seemed to have plenty of energy. Widowed since 1711 by Frederick William, Duke of Courland, she was still living in Annenhof, near Mitau, in dignity and destitution. She had failed to marry Maurice of Saxony, but had recently become enamored of a small landed proprietor in Courland, Johann-Ernest Bühren. During his presentation, Dmitri Golitsyn glossed over this detail and promised that, in any event, if the Supreme Council required it, she would drop her lover without regret and come running back to Russia.

This suggestion seemed to be convincing. Golitsyn then pressed his point, saying, "We agree on Anna Ivanovna. But we should trim her wings a bit!" Golitsyn had in mind subtly reducing the ruler's powers and extending those of the Supreme Privy Council; everyone agreed. The representatives of Russia's oldest families, brought together in a conclave, saw this initiative as a God-sent occasion to reinforce the political influence of the old-stock nobility vis-à-vis the hereditary monarchy and its temporary servants. By this juggling act, they could relieve Her Majesty of a share of the crown, even while pretending to help her adjust it on her head. After a succession of Byzantine discussions, the initiators of this idea agreed that Anna Ivanovna should be recognized as tsarina, but that her prerogative should be limited by a series of conditions to which she must subscribe beforehand.

Upstairs, the members of the Supreme Privy Council removed to the grand salon in the palace, where a multitude of civil, military and ecclesiastical dignitaries awaited the results of their deliberations. Learning of the decision taken by the supreme advisers, Bishop Feofan Prokopovich timidly recollected the will of Catherine I according to which, after the death of Peter II, the crown should revert to his aunt Elizabeth, as a daughter of Peter I and of the late empress. Never mind that the child was born before the parents were married: her mother had transmitted to her the blood of the Romanovs, he said, and nothing else counted when the future of Holy Russia was concerned! Dmitri Golitsyn, indignant at such a speech, shouted, "We will not have any bastards!"[1]

Shocked by this attack, Feofan Prokopovich swallowed his objections; the discussion moved on to a consideration of the "practical conditions." The enumeration of the limits to imperial power ended with an oath to be sworn by the candidate: "If I do not keep these commitments, I agree to forfeit my crown." According to the charter envisaged by the supreme council, the new empress would commit to work to expand the Orthodox faith, not to marry, not to designate an heir and to work closely with the Supreme Privy Council — whose assent would be required in order to declare war, to conclude peace, to raise taxes, to interfere in the affairs of the nobility, to fill key positions in the administration of the empire, to distribute lands, villages, and serfs, and to monitor her personal expenditure of State funds.

This cascade of interdicts astounded the assembly. Wasn't the Council going too far? Weren't they committing a crime of lese-majesty? Those who feared that the powers of the future empress were being reduced without regard for tradition ran afoul of those who were delighted to see this reinforcement of the role of the real boyars in the conduct of Russian political affairs. The second group very quickly drowned out the first. Even the bishop, overwhelmed by the enthusiasm of the majority, kept his mouth shut and ruminated over his fears, alone in a corner. Sure that they had the entire country behind them, the Supreme Privy Council charged Prince Vasily Lukich Dolgoruky, Prince Dmitri Golitsyn and General Leontiev with bearing a message to Anna Ivanovna, in her retirement at Mitau, specifying the conditions under which she would accede to the throne.

Meanwhile, however, Elizabeth Petrovna was being kept abreast of the discussions and the stipulations being bandied about at the Supreme Council. Her doctor and confidant, Armand Lestocq, warned her of the machinations going on in Moscow and begged her "to take action." But she refused to make the least effort to exercise her rights to the succession of Peter II. She had no children and did not wish to have any. In her eyes, her nephew Charles Peter Ulrich, the son of her sister Anna and Duke Charles

Frederick of Holstein, was the legitimate heir. But little Charles Peter Ulrich's mother had died, and the baby was only a few months old. Drowning in sorrow, Elizabeth hesitated to look beyond this mourning. After a number of disappointing adventures, broken engagements, evaporated hopes, she had taken a dislike to the Russian court and preferred the isolation and even the boredom of the countryside to the bustling din and superficial glitter of the palaces.

While she reflected thus, with a melancholy mixed with bitterness, on an imperial future that no longer concerned her, the emissaries of the Council were hastening to bring word to her cousin Anna Ivanovna. She received them with a mocking benevolence. In truth, her spies and the well-wishers that she still had at the court had already informed her of the contents of the letters which the delegation would bring her. Nevertheless, she did not indicate in any way what her intentions might be; without batting an eye, she read the list of rights that the guardians of the regime dictated she should renounce, and said that she would agree to it all. She did not even seem to mind being required to break with her lover, Johann Bühren.

Misled by her dignified and docile air, the plenipotentiaries never suspected that she had already made arrangements to have her favorite join her, in Moscow or St. Petersburg, as soon as she signaled to him that the road was clear. This possibility seemed all the more likely since she was getting word from her partisans in Russia that she had considerable support among the minor nobility. This group was eager to move against the upper aristocracy, the *verkhovniki* as they were popularly called, which they accused of encroaching on the powers of Her Majesty in order to increase their own. Rumors were even circulating that in the event of any conflict, the Imperial Guard, which had always defended the sacred rights of the monarchy, would be disposed to intervene in favor of the descendant of Peter the Great and Catherine I.

Having worked out the details of her secret plan, and having ensured the delegation of her complete subservience, and making a show of bidding Bühren a final good-bye, Anna set out, followed by a retinue worthy of a princess of her rank. On February 10, 1730, she stopped for the night at the village of Vsyesvyatskoye, at the gates of Moscow. Peter II's funeral was to take place the following day. She would not make it in time — and this delay suited her very well. Besides, as she soon heard, a scandal marred the day of mourning. At the last moment Catherine Dolgoruky, the late tsar's fiancée, had demanded that she be given a place in the procession among the members of the imperial family. Those who were truly entitled to this privilege refused to allow her to join them; and after an exchange of invectives, Catherine had gone home, furious. These incidents were reported to Anna Ivanovna in detail; she found it all very amusing. They made the calm and quiet of the village of Vsyesvyatskoye, muffled under a blanket of snow, seem all the more pleasant.

But now she had to direct her thoughts to making her entrance into the former capital of the tsars. Concerned to ensure her popularity, she offered a round of vodka to the detachments of the Preobrazhensky regiment and the Horse Guards who had come to greet her, and forthwith she promoted to colonel the head of these units, Count Simon Andreyevich Saltykov, her principal collaborator, who had been a lieutenant-colonel. By contrast, receiving a courtesy visit from the members of the Supreme Privy Council, she greeted them with frosty correctness; she pretended to be surprised when the chancellor, Gabriel Golovkin, tried to present her with the Order of St. Andrew, which was hers, by right, as sovereign. "It's true," she observed with irony, blocking his gesture, "I had forgotten to take it!" And, calling over one of the men in her entourage, she invited him to hand her the cord,

thus snubbing the chancellor, who was flustered by such contempt for customs. On their way out, the members of the Supreme Privy Council must have been thinking, privately, that this
tsarina was not going to be as easy to handle as they had thought.

On February 15, 1730, Anna Ivanovna finally made her solemn entrance into Moscow and, on the 19th, oaths to Her Majesty
were sworn in the Assumption Cathedral and the main churches
of the city. Having been warned of the Empress's poor opinion of
it, the Supreme Privy Council decided to release some ballast and
to modify somewhat the traditional text of the commitment,
swearing fealty to "Her Majesty and the Empire," which should
calm any apprehensions. Then, after many secret meetings, and
taking into account the uncontrolled maneuverings among the
officers of the Guard, they resigned themselves to softening still
further the wording of the "interdicts" initially envisaged. Enig-
matic and smiling as ever, Anna Ivanovna noted these small cor-
rections without comment. She received her cousin Elizabeth
Petrovna with apparent fondness, accepted her hand-kissing and
affirmed that she felt much solicitude for their common family.
Before dismissing her, she even promised to see to it personally, as
sovereign, that Elizabeth Petrovna would never lack for anything
in her retirement.

However, in spite of this overt subservience and benevolence, she had not lost sight of her goal, in leaving Mitau to return
to Russia. Within the Guard and the lesser and middle nobility,
her partisans were preparing a brilliant deed. On February 25,
1730, she was sitting on her throne, surrounded by the members of
the Supreme Privy Council, with a crowd of courtiers squeezing
around them in the grand salon of the Lefortovo Palace; suddenly,
a few hundred officers of the Guard barged in, with Prince Alexis
Cherkassky, declared champion of the new empress, at their head.
In a rambling speech he struggled to explain that the document

signed by Her Majesty, at the instigation of the Supreme Privy Council, was in contradiction with the principles of the monarchy by divine right. In the name of the million subjects devoted to the cause of Holy Russia, he begged the tsarina to denounce this monstrous act, to convoke the Senate, the nobility, the senior officers, and the church fathers as soon as possible, and to dictate to them her own concept of power.

"We want a tsarina-autocrat, we do not want the Supreme Privy Council!" one of the officers shouted, kneeling before her. Anna Ivanovna, a consummate actress, feigned astonishment. She appeared to have discovered, suddenly, that her good faith had been abused. Believing that she was acting for the good of all in renouncing some of her rights, she now found that she had only done a service to the ambitious and the malicious! "What's this!?" she exclaimed. "When I signed the charter at Mitau, was I not responding to the desires of the entire nation?" And in that moment, the officers of the Guard took a step forward, as if on parade, and exclaimed in unison: "We will not allow laws to be dictated to our sovereign! We are your slaves, but we cannot tolerate rebels taking it upon themselves to control you. Say the word and we will throw their heads at your feet!"

Anna Ivanovna struggled to contain her joy. In a blink of an eye, her triumph repaid all the affronts she had suffered. They thought they could outsmart her, but it was she who had outwitted her sworn enemies, the *verkhovniki*. Glaring at these disloyal dignitaries, she declared: "I do not feel secure here any longer!" And, turning toward the officers, she added: "Obey only Simon Andreyevich Saltykov!"

That was the man whom she had just promoted, a few days before. The windowpanes shook with the officers' cheers. With just one sentence, this able woman had swept away the Supreme Privy Council, thus proving herself worthy of leading Russia to glory, justice and prosperity.

The moment of truth had come. The Empress had the text of the charter read aloud, and after each article, she posed the same question: "Is that what the nation wants?" And, each time, the officers shouted their response: "Long live the sovereign autocrat! Death to the traitors! Death to anyone who refuses her this title!"

Approved by plebiscite even before she was crowned, Anna Ivanovna then concluded, in a sweet tone that contrasted with her imposing matronly stature: "Why, then this paper is useless!" And, to the hurrahs of the crowd, she tore the document to bits and scattered them at her feet.[2]

At the conclusion of this tumultuous event, which she regarded as her real coronation, the Empress and her entourage (still swelled by the officers of the Guard) went to see the members of the Supreme Privy Council — who had preferred to withdraw to another area, rather than watching her moment of triumph. They had thought they were trimming her claws, and here she was slashing them to the quick. Whereas the majority of the councilors were dumb-struck, Dmitri Golitsyn and Vasily Dolgoruky turned to face the mass of their opponents and publicly admitted their defeat. "Let everything be done in accordance with the divine will of Providence!" Dolgoruky said, philosophically.

Again, the crowd burst into cheers. "The Day of Dupes" was over. When it was no longer risky to take sides, Ostermann suddenly emerged. He had pretended to be seriously ill, confined to his room by his doctors; now, bright-eyed and bushy-tailed, he congratulated Anna Ivanovna, swore his unfailing devotion to her and announced, privately, that he was preparing to bring a lawsuit in the name of Her Majesty against the Dolgorukys and the Golitsyns. Anna Ivanovna smiled with a scornful joy. Who thus dared to claim that she was not of the same blood as Peter the Great? She had just proven the opposite. And this idea alone filled her with ride.

The hardest part was over; she could prepare for the coronation without any unnecessary emotion. Striking while the iron was hot, she set the coronation ceremony to take place just two weeks later, on March 15, 1730, with all the usual pomp, in the Assumption Cathedral in the Kremlin. Catherine I, Peter II, Anna Ivanovna: the sovereigns of Russia followed one another at such short intervals that the waltz of "Their Majesties" made everyone dizzy. This empress was the third one in six years to proceed through the streets of Moscow. The novelty was wearing thin, but the crowds still came out to cheer enthusiastically and to proclaim their veneration of their "little mother."

Meanwhile, Anna Ivanovna was not sitting idly by. She started by naming Simon Andreyevich Saltykov, who had served her cause so well, to the post of General-in-Chief and Grand Master of the court; and she relegated to his own domains the far too busy Dmitri Mikhailovich Golitsyn, to do penance there. But most important of all, she hurried to send an emissary to Mitau, where Bühren was impatiently awaiting the good word. He immediately set out for Russia.

In the old capital, meanwhile, the celebrations surrounding the coronation went on, accompanied by gigantic light shows. The scintillating fireworks were soon rivaled by an unusually brilliant aurora borealis. Suddenly, the horizon blazed up. The sky turned radiant, as though it had been injected with blood. Among the people, some dared to call it an ill omen.

Footnotes

1. *Mémoires du prince Dolgoruky*, cited by K. Waliszewski, *L'Héritage de Pierre le Grand*.
2. Details and comments reported in *L'Avènement d'Anna Ire*, by Korsakov; citations quoted in Waliszewski, *op. cit.*

V

THE EXTRAVAGANT ANNA

Married at the age of 17 to Duke Frederick William (who had developed a reputation as a quarrelsome and drunken prince), Anna Ivanovna had retired with her husband to Annenhof, in Courland (today's Lithuania, more or less). A few months after leaving Russia, she found herself widowed. She then moved to Mitau, where she lived in dereliction and embarrassment. During these years when the whole world seemed to have forgotten her very existence, she had a constant companion in Ernst Johann Bühren, a petty nobleman from Westphalia. A man of little education but unlimited ambition, Bühren replaced her first lover, Peter Bestuzhev. He proved to be very effective at the day's work, in the office, and at night, in Anna's bed. She accepted his guidance as readily as his caresses; and he relieved her of all her worries and provided all the pleasure she could wish for. Although his real name was Bühren, and although his family and friends had Russianized it to Biren, he preferred a "Frenchified" version — Biron. He was a grandson of one of Jacques de Courland's stablemen, but that did not stop him from pretending to a very honorable heritage; he claimed to be related to the noble French family, de Biron.

Anna Ivanovna took him at his word. Moreover, she was so attached to him that she discovered hundreds of similarities in the way they both approached life; this harmony of tastes went as far as the details of their intimate behavior. Like his imperial mistress, Bühren adored luxury but was none too scrupulous when it came to moral or bodily purity. A woman of horse sense and robust health, Anna was not offended by anything and even appreciated Bühren's odor of sweat and cattle sheds, and the Teutonic roughness of his language. At the table as in bed, she preferred substantial satisfactions and strong scents. She liked to eat, she liked to drink, she liked to laugh. A very large woman with a well-rounded belly and an ample bust, her body, weighed down with fat, was topped by a bloated, puffy face crowned by abundant brown hair and lit up by eyes of a sharp blue, whose boldness disarmed people before she even spoke. She was mad for brilliantly-colored dresses trimmed with gilt thread and embroidery; and she had little use for the aromatic toilette waters in use at the court. Among her entourage, it was said that she insisted on cleansing her skin with melted butter.

She took pride in having as many horses as there are days in the year. Every morning, she would inspect her stables and kennels with all the satisfaction of a miser inventorying his treasure — but she was full of contradictions. While she adored animals, she also took a sadistic pleasure in killing them and even torturing them. Soon after accepting the crown and being installed in St. Petersburg, she ordered that loaded rifles be kept in every room of the Winter Palace. Sometimes she would be struck by an irresistible impulse — cracking open a window, she would snap up her weapon and shoot a bird out of the sky. As the salons shook with the explosion and filled with gun-smoke, she would call her startled ladies in waiting and order them to do the same, under penalty of being dismissed.

She also enjoyed Dutch humming-tops and she would have her representative in Amsterdam buy bundles of the special string out of which the whips were made for spinning the tops. She exhibited the same passion for silks and trinkets, which she would order from France. She was fond of performances of any kind. Everything that flatters the spirit, everything that tickles the senses, was charming to her.

On the other hand, she did not see any need to cultivate learning by reading books or listening to the discourses of alleged specialists. Greedy and lazy, she went along according to her instincts and utilized the briefest leisure moments to take naps. Having drowsed for an hour or so, she would call in Bühren, negligently sign whatever papers he put before her and, having thus fulfilled her imperial obligations, she would open the door and hail the young ladies of honor who sat in the next room sewing embroideries.

"*Nu, dyevki, poïti!* [OK, girls, give us a song!]," she would cry.

Her docile followers would strike up the choir, singing some popular refrain, and she would listen to them with a happy smile, nodding her head. This interlude would go on as long as the singers were able to more or less keep up a pretense of following the tune. If one of them, overcome by fatigue, lowered her voice or hit a wrong note, Anna Ivanovna would correct her with a resounding roar. Often, she would call storytellers to her bedside, and have them entertain her with the tales she had enjoyed in her childhood, always the same ones; or she would call in a monk who was good at explaining the truths of religion. Another obsession which she flattered herself with having inherited from Peter the Great was her passion for grotesque exhibitions and natural monstrosities. Nothing was funnier to her than the spectacles performed by buffoons and dwarves. The uglier and stupider they were, the more she applauded their jokes and antics. After 19 years of provincial mediocrity and obscurity, she wanted to remove the veneer of propriety and impose on the court a life of unprecedented luxury and chaos. Nothing struck her as too beautiful nor too expensive — when it came to satisfying the whims of the sovereign.

However, this Russia that accident had given her to rule was not, strictly speaking, her fatherland. And she hardly saw the need to make it her own. Certainly, she had some good old Russian families in her pocket including, among the most devoted, old Gabriel Golovkin, the Trubestkoy princes and Ivan Baryatinsky, Paul Yaguzhinsky (that famous hot-head), and the impulsive Alexis Cherkassky, whom she made her chancellor. But the reins were in the hands of the Germans. The empire's policies were set by a team composed entirely of men of Germanic origin, taking orders from the terrible Bühren.

The old boyars, so proud of their genealogy, were swept from center stage when Her Majesty and her favorite came into power. Coming from backgrounds in the civil administration as well as the military, the new bigshots of the regime included the Loewenwolde brothers, Baron von Brevern, the Generals Rodolph von Bismarck and Christoph von Manstein, and Field Marshal Burkhard von Münnich. A four-man cabinet replaced the Supreme Privy Council and Ostermann, in spite of his ambiguous past, still served as Prime Minister; but it was Ernst Johann Bühren, the Empress's favorite, who chaired the meetings and made the final decisions.

Impervious to the concept of pity, never hesitating to send a troublemaker to the dungeon, to Siberia or to the torture chambers for a good thrashing, Bühren did not even need to ask Anna

Ivanovna's opinion before dictating these punishments, for he knew in advance that she would approve them. Was if because she actually had the same opinion as her lover, in so many instances, that she left him such a free hand — or was it simply because she was too lazy to oppose him? The people who had to deal with Bühren unanimously commented on the hardness of his face, which seemed to be carved from stone, and the look in his eye — like a bird of prey. One word from him could make all of Russia happy or desperate. His mistress did nothing more than lend her imprimatur to all that he did. And, like her, he was avid for luxury, and he took full advantage of his almost-kingly position to accept bribes right and left. He expected payment for the least service rendered.

His contemporaries found his cupidity to exceed even that of Menshikov, but it was not this systematic misappropriation that bothered them most. The preceding reigns had accustomed them to greasing the wheels. No, it was the excessive Germanization that Bühren was introducing into their fatherland that irritated them more each day. Admittedly, Anna Ivanovna had always spoken and written German better than Russian, but since Bühren took over the highest level in the hierarchy, it seemed that in fact the entire State apparatus had changed. If someone of Russian stock had been committing these crimes, thefts, and abuses or granting favors the way this arrogant parvenu was doing, Her Majesty's subjects would have found it easier to swallow. But the fact that these liberties were taken or tolerated by a foreigner made them seem twice as bad to the victims. Boiling with rage over the conduct of this tyrant who was not even one of their own, the Russians invented a word for the regime of terror that he imposed on them — behind his back, they talked about the "Bironovschina"[1] as is it were a killer epidemic that was plaguing the country. Records of illicit payments exist that prove this name was justified.

For daring to stand up to the tsarina and her favorite, Prince Ivan Dolgoruky was drawn and quartered; his two uncles, Sergei and Ivan, were decapitated, and another member of the family, Vasily Lukich, a former participant in the Supreme Privy Council, met the same fate, while Catherine Dolgoruky, former fiancée of Peter, was shut away in a convent for life.

While eliminating his former rivals and those who might be tempted to take over where they had left off, Bühren worked to add to his personal titles, which he felt should keep pace with his increasing wealth. When Duke Ferdinand of Courland died on April 23, 1737, he sent Russian regiments under the command of General Bismarck[2] to Mitau, "to intimidate" the Courland Diet and encourage it to elect him, disregarding any other candidate that might exist. Over the protests of the Teutonic Order, Ernst Johann Bühren was proclaimed, as he demanded, Duke of Courland. He intended to run this Russian province by remote control, from St. Petersburg. Moreover, Charles VI, emperor of Germany, gave him the title of count of the Holy Empire; and he managed to have himself designated a knight of St. Alexander and St. Alexis. There was no honor or princely prerogative to which he did not lay claim. Anyone in Russia who wanted to get ahead, in any endeavor whatsoever, had to go through him.

Courtiers have always regarded it as an honor and a privilege to be admitted to the ruler's private rooms. Now, stepping into the Empress's bedroom, visitors would find Her Majesty still in her nightgown, with the inevitable Bühren lying at her side. Protocol required that the new arrival, even if he was a high-ranking official, kiss the hand that the sovereign held out to him above the bedcovers. To secure the good graces of her lover, as well, some took the opportunity to kiss his hand with same respectful air. And there were even some flatterers who extended the standards of etiquette to the point of kissing Her Majesty's bare foot. And it has been alleged that, deep in the recesses of the imperial apartments, one Alexis Miliutin, a simple coal shoveler (*istopnik*) who, tending the stove in Anna Ivanovna's room every morning, felt compelled to devoutly brush the tsarina's and her companion's feet with his lips. In reward for this daily homage, the *istopnik* was given a nobleman's title. However, to preserve a trace of his modest origins, he was constrained use fireplace tools as the blazon on his coat of arms.[3]

On Sundays, Anna Ivanovna's six favorite clowns had orders to line up outside the great dining room at the end of the dinner that was attended by all the members of the court. When the Empress and her retinue walked out, on their way back to church, the buffoons would squat side by side, imitating hens laying eggs and making comical noises. To make things even funnier, they had their faces smeared with coal and were ordered to roughhouse, and to scratch and fight until they drew blood. At the sight of these capers, the inspirer of the game and her faithful followers howled with laughter. And Her Majesty's buffoons were too well paid to complain.

The descendants of the great families, including Alexis Petrovich Apraxin, Nikita Fyodorovich Volkonsky and even Mikhail Alexeyevich Golitsyn joined in. The tone was set by the professional jester, Balakirev, but whenever he was slow to come up with new tricks, the Empress would have him beaten to revive his inspiration. Then there was the violonist Peter Mira Pedrillo, who would scratch at his squeaky fiddle while prancing around like a monkey; and D'Acosta, the Jewish Portuguese polyglot who would egg on his accomplices by whipping them. The poor poet Trediakovsky, having composed an erotic and burlesque poem, was invited to read it before Her Majesty. He describes this literary event in a letter: "I had the pleasure of reading my verses before Her Imperial Majesty and, after the reading, I had the distinguished favor of receiving a gracious slap from Her Imperial Majesty's own hand."[4]

However, the mainstays of the comic troop around Balakirev were the freaks and dwarves of both genders; they were known by their nicknames: Beznozhka (the woman with no legs), Gorbushka (the hunchback). The tsarina's fascination with physical hideousness and mental aberration was, she maintained, her way of showing interest in the mysteries of nature. Following the example of her grandfather Peter the Great, she claimed that studying the malformations of human beings helped her to understand the structure and the operation of normal bodies and minds. Surrounding herself with monsters was just another way of serving science. Moreover, according to Anna Ivanovna, the spectacle of other people's misfortunes would reinforce everyone's desire to look after his health.

Among the gallery of human monstrosities of which the empress was so proud, one of her favorites was a stunted old Kalmyk woman who was so ugly that even the priests were afraid of her. No one could make funnier faces. One day the Kalmyk exclaimed, as a joke, that she would like to marry. In a flash of inspiration, the tsarina thought of a wonderful trick. While all the members of the small troop of court buffoons were experts at clowning around, not all of them were, strictly speaking, deformed — for instance, the old nobleman, Mikhail Alexeyevich Golitsyn, who held a sinecure as "imperial jester." He had been a widower for a few years. Suddenly he was informed that Her Majesty had found a new wife for him and that, in her extreme kindness, she was ready to take care of all the arrangements and to cover all the expenses of the wedding. The Empress was famous as an "indefatigable matchmaker," so that no further explanation was needed. However, the preparations for this union looked to be unusual at the very least. According to the tsarina's instructions, the Cabinet Minister, Artyom Volynsky, had a vast house hastily built on the Neva embankment between the Winter Palace and the Admiralty, out of blocks of ice that were welded together by dribbling water in between them. The house was 60 feet long, over 20 feet wide, and 30 feet high, and was topped by a gallery with colonnade and statues. A staircase with a balustrade led to a vestibule, behind which the apartment reserved for the couple was located. It held a room furnished with a great white bed, whose curtains, pillows and mattress were carved of ice. To the side was a bathroom, also cut from ice, as evidence of Her Majesty's concern for the intimate necessities on behalf of her "protégés." Further on was a dining room, of similarly polar aspect but richly furnished in formal china and tableware, ready to welcome the guests for a superb and shivery and feast. In front of the house stood ice cannons, with a stack of cannonballs of the same material, and an ice elephant that was said to be able to spit a stream of frosty water 24 feet into the air, plus two ice pyramids inside of which were exhibited, to warm up the visitors, some humorous and obscene images. [5]

Her Majesty expressly invited representatives of all the races of the empire, dressed in their native costumes, to participate in the great festival given in honor of the marriage of the buffoons. On February 6, 1740, after the unfortunate Mikhail Golitsyn and the counterfeit old Kalmyk woman had their ritual blessing at the church, a carnival procession similar to those that had so amused Peter the Great set forth to the clanging of bells. Ostiak, Kirghiz, Finn, Samoyed, Yakut — they all filed along, proud in their traditional clothes, parading down the street. The crowds who had come running from every part of the city to enjoy this free spectacle were flabbergasted. Some of the participants rode horses of a species never before seen in St. Petersburg, others rode in reindeer-drawn sledges or dog-sleds, on the back of a goat or, more hilarious yet, on the back of a pig. The newlyweds themselves were seated on an elephant. After passing in front of the imperial palace, the procession stopped across from the "Duke of Courland's Riding School," where a meal was served for all the participants. The poet Trediakovsky recited a comic poem and couples from the different regions performed folk dances, accompanied by their traditional instruments, for the benefit of the Empress, the court and the "young couple."

As night was finally falling, they all set out again, in good cheer but still with their wits about them, toward the house of ice which, in the lengthening shadows of twilight, sparkled with the gleam of a thousand torches. Her Majesty Herself took care to escort the newlyweds to their cold bed and withdrew with a ribald smile. Sentries were placed in front of all the exits, at once, to prevent the turtledoves from leaving their icy love nest before daybreak.

That night, while lying with Bühren in her well-heated room, Anna Ivanovna appreciated more than ever her soft bedcovers and warm clothes. Did she even think of the ugly Kalmyk and the docile Golitsyn, whom she had condemned capriciously to this sinister comedy and who might well have been dying of cold in their translucent prison? In any event, if any hint of remorse flitted through her mind, it must have been driven out very quickly by the thought that this was quite an innocent joke and very much in line with the liberties that are allowed any sovereign, by divine right.

By some miracle, the noble buffoon and his hideous partner were, according to a few contemporaries, pulled out of this matrimonial ice cube with nothing worse than a runny nose and some frostbite. According to some, they even managed to go abroad, under the following reign, where the Kalmyk supposedly died after having given birth to two sons. As for Golitsyn, by no means discouraged by this chilling matrimonial test, he was said to have married again and to have lived on to a very advanced age, without any further misadventures. Diehard monarchists thus maintain that even the worst atrocities committed in Russia in the name of the autocracy of that era could only have been beneficial.

In spite of Anna Ivanovna's obvious indifference to public affairs, Bühren was sometimes constrained to acquaint her with important issues. In order to better insulate her from the annoyances that are inseparable from the exercise of power, he suggested to her that they create a secret chancellery that would be responsible for monitoring Her subjects. Fed by the public treasury, an army of spies was let loose throughout Russia. Denouncements popped up on all sides, like mushrooms after a sweet rainfall.

Informers wishing to express themselves verbally were let into the imperial palace by a hidden door and were received, in the offices of the secret chancellery, by Bühren in person. His innate hatred for the old Russian aristocracy encouraged him to accept without question any accusations against members of that caste. The more highly placed the culprit, the more the "Favorite" enjoyed precipitating his downfall. Under his reign, the torture rooms were seldom vacant and not a week went by in which he did not sign orders exiling someone to Siberia or relegating someone to a remote province, for life. In the specialized administrative department of the *Sylka* (Deportation), the employees, overwhelmed by the burgeoning files, often expedited defendants to the ends of the earth without taking the time to verify their guilt, or even their identity.

To prevent any protest against this blind rigor on the part of the legal authorities, Bühren created a new regiment of the Guard, the Ismailovsky Regiment, and gave the command not to a Rus-

sian soldier (they were wary of them, at the top!), but to a Baltic
nobleman, Karl Gustav Loewenwolde, the brother of the Grand
Master of the court, Reinhold Loewenwolde. This elite unit
joined the Semyonovsky and Preobrazhensky regiments in order
to supplement the forces available for maintaining law and order.
Their instructions were simple: every living person within the
country must be rendered incapable of doing harm. The most famous dignitaries were, on the basis of their prominence in itself,
the most highly suspect in the view of the chancellery's hench-
men. It was practically a crime not to have German or Baltic ancestors in one's lineage.

Frightened and indignant, Anna Ivanovna's subjects certainly considered Bühren responsible for these evils, but they also
blamed the tsarina. The boldest dared to mutter among themselves that a woman is congenitally unable to govern an empire
and that the curse inherent in her gender had been communicated
to the Russian nation, guilty of imprudently entrusting its destiny
to her.

Even the errors of international politics were blamed on her;
of course, that was actually Ostermann's area of responsibility.
This character of such limited capability and such unlimited ambition was cocksure of his diplomatic genius. His initiatives in
this field cost the country dearly. For one thing, in order to please
Austria, he intervened in Poland — thus making trouble with
France, favored the candidature of Stanislaw Leszczynski. Then,
after the crowning of Augustus III, he thought it would be an astute maneuver to swear never to partition the country; this did
not convince anyone and did not earn him any gratitude. Moreover, counting on support from Austria — which as usual would
let him down — he went to war with Turkey. Münnich achieved
a series of successes on the battlefield, but the losses were so
heavy that Ostermann was constrained to sign a peace accord. At

the Congress of Belgrade, in 1739, he even asked France to mediate — meanwhile trying to bribe the envoy from Versailles — but the results he obtained were contemptible: he managed to hang onto Russia's rights in the Azov peninsula, with the proviso that the area not be fortified, and he gained a few acres of steppe between the Dniepr and the southernmost Bug. In exchange, Russia promised to demolish the fortifications at Taganrog and to give up its merchant fleet and warships in the Black Sea, leaving all free navigation to the Turkish fleet. Russia's only territorial gain during Anna's reign was the effective annexation of Ukraine, which was placed under Russian control in 1734.

Internationally, Russia was seen as a weak and disoriented nation, but inside the country new and absurd aspirants to the throne were cropping up everywhere. This phenomenon was nothing new. Since the epidemic of false Dmitris appeared at the death of Ivan the Terrible, the obsession with miraculously resurrected tsareviches had become an endemic and national disease. Nevertheless, this turmoil in public opinion, however ludicrous it might be, was starting to disturb Anna Ivanovna. She saw the trend as an increasingly specific threat to her legitimacy, and Bühren encouraged that view.

She feared above all that her aunt Elizabeth Petrovna might have a belated renewal of popularity, since she was the sole living daughter of Peter the Great. There was a chance that among the nobility the same specious arguments that (thankfully) had failed to compromise her own coronation might enjoy a resurgence, and not so innocuously this time. Moreover, she found her rival's beauty and natural grace intolerable. It was not enough for her to eject the tsarevna from the palace in the hope that the court, and everyone else, would end up forgetting all about this spoilsport. To forestall any attempt to transfer power to another lineage, she even thought, in 1731, of an authoritative modification of the fam-

ily rights in the house of Romanov. Having no child of her own
and being extremely concerned over the future of the monarchy,
she adopted her young niece, the only daughter of her elder sister
Catherine Ivanovna and Charles Leopold, prince of Mecklenburg.

The little princess was brought to Russia in the twinkling of
an eye. The gamine was only 13 years old at the time. Lutheran by
confession, she was re-baptized as an Orthodox and had her first
name changed from Elizabeth to Anna Leopoldovna; she became
the second most eminent figure in the empire, after her aunt Anna
Ivanovna. She grew into an insipid teenager with a fair complexion; there wasn't much sparkle in her eye, but she had enough
brains to manage a conversation (provided that the subject was
not too serious). As soon as she reached the age of 19, her aunt,
the tsarina, who was a good judge of a woman's physical and
moral resources, decreed that she was ready for marriage. Suitable prospects were hastily sought.

Of course, Anna Ivanovna turned her attention first toward
what she liked to think of as her homeland, Germany. That land
of discipline and virtue was the only place to find husbands and
wives worthy of reigning over barbarian Muscovy. Charged with
discovering a *rara avis* amidst the flocks of crowing roosters, Karl
Gustav Loewenwolde went out to see what he could see. Upon
his return, he recommended either Margrave Charles of Prussia or
Prince Anthony Ulrich of Bevern, of the house of Brunswick,
brother-in-law of the crown prince in Prussia. Personally, he was
inclined in favor of the second candidate, whereas Ostermann,
with his special interest in foreign relations, was inclined toward
the first. The advantages and disadvantages of the two champions
were debated before Anna Ivanovna, without consulting the interested party who would, however, have her word to say, for she
was already over the age of 20.

To tell the truth, the empress had only one goal in all this political-marital machination: to have her niece bring a child into the world as soon as possible, in order to make it heir to the crown, which would cut short any maneuvers by external parties. But who would be more likely to impregnate sweet Anna Leopoldovna faster, Charles of Prussia or Prince Anthony Ulrich? Hesitating, they had Anthony Ulrich brought in to be presented to Her Majesty. One glance was enough for the Empress to evaluate the applicant: a decent young man, polished, weak. Certainly not appropriate for her niece — nor for the country, for that matter. But the omniscient Bühren was anxious to build him up. And time was of the essence, for the girl was not sitting idle, herself. She had recently fallen in love with Count Charles Maurice of Lynar, Saxon minister at St. Petersburg. Fortunately, the king of Saxony had recalled the diplomat and posted him to another station. Heartbroken, Anna Leopoldovna immediately threw herself into another passion. This time, it was a woman: Baroness Julie Mengden. They quickly became inseparable. How far did they take their intimacy? They were the chief butt of gossip at the court and in the embassies; "a lover's passion for a new mistress is nothing, compared to this," noted the English minister Edward Finch.[6] On the other hand, the Prussian minister Axel of Mardefeld was more skeptical; he wrote to his king, in French: "Nobody can understand the source of the Grand Duchess's [Anna Leopoldovna] supernatural attraction to Juliette [Julie Mengden]; so I am not surprised that the public accuses this girl of following the tastes of the famous Sapho. . . . a black calumny, . . . for the late empress, on similar charges, made this young lady undergo a rigorous examination, . . . and the commission's report was favorable in that they found that she is a girl in every part, without any appearance of maleness [sic]."[7]

Given the danger that this deviant love represented, Anna Ivanovna decided that it was time to take action. A bad marriage would be better than a prolonged delay. As for the virgin's tender feelings, Her Majesty laughed them off. This little person, whose grace and innocence had charmed her at first, had become annoying over the years; she had become demanding, and had a disappointingly obstinate temperament. Certainly, she had adopted Anna not to make her happy, as she had claimed hundreds of times, but to put more distance between the throne and Tsarevna Elizabeth Petrovna, whom she hated. Anna Leopoldovna's only value in her eyes was as a smokescreen, a last resort, or a convenient womb to be used. So let her settle for someone like Anthony Ulrich for husband! Even that was too good for an airhead like her!

Despite the fiancée's tears, the wedding took place on July 14, 1739. The majestic ball that followed the bridal blessing bedazzled even the most bilious diplomats. The bride wore a gown of silver thread, heavily embroidered. A diamond crown shone with the light of a thousand flames in her thick dark hair, with luscious braids. However, she was not the star of the ball. In her fairytale toilette, she looked out of place in this company. Among all the joyful faces, hers was marked by melancholy and resignation. And she was eclipsed by the beauty, the smile and the poise of the Tsarevna Elizabeth Petrovna who, according to protocol, had to be invited to temporarily come out of retirement at Ismailovo. Dressed in a gown of rose and silver, very much décolleté, and scintillating with her mother's jewels (the late Empress Catherine I), it seemed as though it was she, and not the bride, who was enjoying the most wonderful day of her life. Even Anthony Ulrich, the brand new husband so little appreciated by Anna Leopoldovna, had eyes only for the tsarevna, the unwanted guest, whose defeat this ceremony was supposed to confirm. Obliged to observe her rival's triumph, hour after hour, the tsarina's hatred only grew. This creature that she thought she had cut down was still rearing its head.

As for Anna Leopoldovna, she suffered like a martyr, knowing she was only a puppet with her aunt pulling the strings. What distressed her most of all was the prospect of what awaited her in bed, after the candelabra were extinguished and the dancers had dispersed. An expiatory victim, she understood very well that while all these people were pretending to be happy over her good fortune, nobody was in fact concerned about her feelings, nor even her pleasure. She was not there to be happy, but to be inseminated.

When the so-dreaded moment arrived, the highest ladies and the wives of the leading foreign diplomats accompanied Anna Leopoldovna, in procession, to the bridal suite to participate in the traditional "bedding of the bride." This was not exactly the same ceremony as that which Anna Ivanovna had imposed on her two buffoons, condemned to freeze all night in the "house of ice"; and yet, the effect was the same for the young woman, forcibly married. She was shaken to the bone, not by cold but by fear, at the thought of the sad destiny that awaited her with a man that she did not love. When the ladies in her retinue finally withdrew, she gave in to deep panic and, giving the slip to her chambermaids, she fled to the gardens of the Summer Palace. And there, in tears, she spent the first night of her married life.

Hearing of this scandalous marital truancy, the tsarina and Bühren called in the poor girl and, preaching, reasoning, begging and threatening, demanded that she carry through at the first opportunity. Sequestered in the next room, a few young ladies of honor observed the scene through a crack in the door. At the height of the discussion, they saw the tsarina, flushed with anger, slap her recalcitrant niece full in the face.

The lesson bore fruit: one year later, on August 23, 1740, Anna gave birth to a son. He was immediately baptized as Ivan

Antonovich (son of Anthony).   The tsarina, who for several months had been suffering from a vague ailment that the doctors were hesitant to put a name to, was suddenly reinvigorated by "the great news." Transported with joy, she required that all Russia rejoice in this providential birth. As always, accustomed to obey and make believe, her subjects celebrated riotously.

But among them, several prudent thinkers asked themselves by what right a brat of thoroughly German origin (since he was Brunswick-Bevern by his father, and Mecklenburg-Schwerin by his mother), and whose only connection to the Romanov dynasty was through his great-aunt Catherine I, wife of Peter the Great (herself of Polish-Livonian origin), should be promoted right from the cradle to the rank of true heir to the Russian crown? By virtue of what law, what national tradition was the Tsarina Anna Ivanovna assuming the power to designate her successor? How could it be that she had no advisor at her side with enough respect for the history of Russia to hold her back from taking such a sacrilegious initiative? However, as usual, they kept these offensive comments to themselves, not wishing to run afoul of Bühren who, although he was German too, claimed to know better than any Russian what was appropriate for Russia.

At one time, he had vaguely thought of marrying his own son, Peter, to Anna Leopoldovna. This plan had failed because of the princess's recent union with Anthony Ulrich; now, the favorite was anxious to ensure indirectly his future as acting Head of State. He considered it all the more urgent to advance his pawns on the chessboard since Her Majesty's health was worsening by the day. There was a concern that she was suffering from a complicated renal impairment due to the effects of "being over the hill." The doctors talked of "stones."

Despite her sufferings, the tsarina still had periods of lucidity. Bühren took advantage of this to ask one last favor: to be named Regent of the empire until the child — who had been just proclaimed heir to the throne — came to majority. This brazen request unleashed the indignation of the dying empress's other councilors: Loewenwolde, Ostermann and Münnich. They were soon joined in their palace plot by Cherkassky and Bestuzhev. After hours of secret discussions, they agreed that the greatest danger ahead was by no means their compatriot Bühren, but the clique of Russian aristocrats, who still had not accepted being brushed aside. In the final analysis, they reckoned, given the danger that some champion of the old-stock nobility would make an attempt to seize power, it would be preferable, for the German clan, to support their dear old accomplice Bühren. Thus, these five confederates (three of whom were of Germanic origin while the two others had ties to foreign courts) decided to place the destiny of the empire in the hands of a character who had never shown any concern for the traditions of Russia and who had not even taken the trouble to learn the language of the country that he claimed to govern. Having come to this resolve, they so advised Bühren — who had never doubted that they would see things his way.

Now they were all reconciled, united around a common interest, and they strove to convince the empress. Rocked between bouts of pain and delusion, she never left her bed anymore. She must hardly have been able to hear Bühren as he tried to explain to her what he wanted: a simple signature at the bottom of a page. Since she seemed too tired to answer him, he slipped the document under her pillow. Surprised by this gesture, she whispered, "Do you need that?" Then she turned her head and refused to speak anymore.

A few days later, Bestuzhev drafted another declaration, by which the Senate and the Generalité implored Her Majesty to entrust the regency to Bühren, in order to ensure the continuation of the empire "under whatever circumstance may arise." Once more, the patient left the paper under her pillow without deigning to initial it — nor even to read it. Bühren and "his men" were dismayed by this inertia — which was likely to be final. Would they have to resort again to forgery to avoid trouble? What had happened on January 1730 when the young tsar Peter II had died was not encouraging.* Considering the ill will of the nobility, it would be dangerous to repeat that game with every change of reign.

However, on October 16, 1740, the tsarina took a turn for the better. She called in her old favorite and, with a trembling hand, gave him the signed document. Finally, Bühren could breathe again — and with him, all those in the close band who had contributed to this victory *in extremis*. The new regent's partisans hoped that their efforts, more or less spontaneous, would be repaid before long, While Her Majesty was on her death bed, they counted the days and calculated the coming rewards. The priest was called in, and the prayer for the dying was said. Lulled by the chanting, she cast her eye about and, in her distress, recognized through her fog the tall silhouette of Münnich among those in attendance. She smiled to him as if beseeching his protection for the one who would one day be taking her place on the throne of Russia, and murmured, "Good-bye, Field Marshal!" Later, she added, "Good-bye, everyone!" These were her last words. She slipped into a coma on October 28, 1740.

At the announcement of her death, Russia shook off a nightmare. But around the palace, the expectation was that the nation might be falling into an even blacker horror. The imperial court was unanimous in its opinion that, with a nine-month-old tsar still in his crib and a regent of German origin (who could express himself in Russian only reluctantly and whose principal concern

---

*Vasily Lukich Dolgoruky, for one, was executed in the wake of that event.

was to destroy the country's noblest families), the empire was heading straight for a catastrophe.

The day after Anna Ivanovna's death, Bühren became regent by the grace of the recently departed, with a baby as his mascot and as the living guarantee of his rights. He immediately set himself to clearing the ground around him. In his view, the first essential move would be to get rid of Anna Leopoldovna and Anthony Ulrich, little Ivan's parents. If he could send them far enough from the capital — and why not abroad? — he would have his free hands until the imperial brat attained his majority. Studying the new political aspect of Russia, Baron Axel of Mardefeld, Prussian Minister to St. Petersburg, summarized his opinion on the future of the country in a dispatch to his sovereign Frederick II, saying: "Seventeen years of despotism [the legal duration of the minority of the tsar] and a nine-month-old child who, by the way, could die, yielding the throne to the regent."[8]

Mardefeld's letter is dated October 29, 1740, the day following the death of the tsarina. Less than a week later, events suddenly took a turn in a direction that the diplomat had not foreseen. Despite the future tsar Ivan VI's being transferred to the Winter Palace amid great pomp and celebration, in an extravagant ceremony followed by all the courtiers swearing their oath and kissing the hand of the regent, his enemies had not given up.

The new English minister in St. Petersburg, Edward Finch, declared that the change of reign "has made less noise in Russia than the changing of the Guard in Hyde Park"; but Field Marshal Münnich warned Anna Leopoldovna and Anthony Ulrich against the tortuous machinations of Bühren, who he suggested was intending to throw them both out in order to keep himself in power. Even though he had been allied with the regent in the very recent past, he said that he felt morally obliged to prevent him from going any further to the detriment of the legitimate rights of the family. According to him, for his next coup d'état, the ex-favorite of the late empress Anna Ivanovna was counting on the Is- mailovsky Regiment and the horse guard, one of which was under the command of his brother Gustav, the other under his son. But the Preobrazhensky Regiment was entirely at the behest of the field marshal and this elite unit would be disposed to act, at the proper time, against the ambitious Bühren. "If Your Highness wishes," Münnich told the princess, "I would relieve you of this treacherous man in one hour."[9]

However, Anna Leopoldovna had no stomach for such ad- ventures. Frightened at the thought of attacking a man as power- ful and cunning as Bühren, she balked. However, having con- sulted her husband, she changed her mind and decided, while some trembling, to play all or nothing. During the night of No- vember 8, 1740, a hundred grenadiers and three officers of the Preobrazhensky Regiment, sent by Münnich, burst into the room where Bühren was sleeping; they yanked him out of bed and, de- spite his cries for help, they beat him with their rifle butts and carried him out, semi-conscious, to an enclosed carriage. In the wee hours of the day, he was transported to the Schlüsselburg Fortress on Lake Ladoga, where he was methodically whipped. They needed a charge that could be substantiated before they could have him imprisoned, so he was accused of precipitating the death of the empress by having her ride on horseback at the wrong time. Other crimes, added to this one at the appropriate time, were enough to have him condemned to death on April 8, 1741. First, he was to be drawn and quartered, but his sentence was commuted immediately to exile in perpetuity to a remote vil- lage in Siberia; and in one fell swoop, Anna Leopoldovna was pro- claimed regent.

To celebrate the happy end of this period of intrigues, usur- pations and treason, she rescinded the preceding government's ban on soldiers' and warrant officers' visiting cabarets. This first liberal measure was greeted by an outburst of joy in the barracks — and in the bars. Everyone hoped this was a sign of broader leniency in general. The name of the new regent was blessed everywhere and, with hers, that of the man who had just brought her to power. Only the mean-spirited happened to notice that Bühren was being replaced by Münnich. One German was taking the place of another, without any concern for Muscovite tradition. How long would the empire have to endure a foreign master? And why was it always a member of the weaker sex that came to occupy the throne? Was there no other choice for Russia but to be ruled by an empress, with Germans at her back, whispering in her ear? Sad as it may be for a country to smother under a woman's skirts, how much worse it is when that woman herself is under the influence of a foreigner. The most pessimistic observers reckoned that Russia would be threatened with a double calamity as a long as real men and real Russians did not stand up against the reign of besotted sovereigns and German lovers. These prophets of gloom saw the matriarchy and the Prussian takeover as two facets of a curse that had befallen the fatherland since the demise of Peter the Great.

Footnotes

1. The "Frenchified" version of his name, plus a pejorative ending, was used to indicate the excesses committed by Bühren and his clique.
2. Ancestor of Bismarck, the "Iron Chancellor."
3. His great-grandson Dmitri Miliutin, War Minister under Alexander II, would retain these evocative emblems on his blazon.
4. Cf. Brian-Chaninov, *op. cit.*
5. Cf. Kraft: *Description de la maison de glace*, and K. Waliszewski, *op. cit.*
6. Cf. Daria Oliver, *op. cit.*
7. Letter dated 10 December 1740, cited by K. Waliszewski, *op. cit.*
8. Cf. Brian-Chaninov, *op. cit.*
9. Comments reported in K. Waliszewski, *op. cit.*

VI

One Anna after Another

Still dazed by her sudden accession to power, Anna Leopoldovna was not so much interested in her political triumph as
in the return to St. Petersburg of her last lover, whom the tsarina
thought she had skillfully removed from the picture by marrying
Anna to the insipid Anthony Ulrich. As soon as the coast was
clear, the count of Lynar returned, ready for the most exciting adventures. Casting her eyes upon him once again, she fell under his
spell instantly. He hadn't changed a bit in the months of separation. At the age of 40, he looked barely 30. Tall and slender, with
a fine complexion and sparkling eyes, he always wore clothes in
soft colors — sky blue, apricot or lilac — and used plenty of
French perfumes and a pomade to keep his hands soft. They said
he was an Adonis in his prime, or a Narcissus who never aged.
There is no doubt that Anna Leopoldovna made her bed available
to him again immediately; and there is no doubt either that Anthony Ulrich accepted this sharing arrangement without blinking
an eye. No one at the court was surprised by this eternal triangle,
which they had immediately suspected would be reconstituted.

Besides, Russian and foreign observers alike noted that the regent's renewed passion for Lynar by no means diminished the ardor that she continued to feel for her close friend Julie Mengden. That she was able to appreciate the traditional pleasure of the relationship between an woman and a man as much as the ambiguous savor of a relationship with a partner of her own sex was all to her honor, in the opinion of the libertines, for such eclecticism is evidence of both broadmindedness and a generous temperament.

An indolent daydreamer, she would spend long hours lying in bed. She would get up late, trail around in her private chambers, scantily dressed and hair barely done, reading novels that she would drop halfway through, and making the sign of the cross twenty times over before the many icons that she had placed on her walls — the zeal of a convert. She insisted that love and recreation were the only *raisons d'etre* of a woman of her age.

This casual behavior did not bother her entourage, neither her husband nor his ministers. A regent who was more concerned about the goings on in her bedroom than in her State suited them very well. Admittedly, from time to time, in his wounded pride Anthony Ulrich would make a show of being the indignant husband, but his tantrums were so artificial and so brief that Anna Leopoldovna only laughed at him. These fake marital scenes even encouraged her to intensify her dissipation, as a way of teasing him.

However, while continuing his assiduous attentions to her, Lynar was not indifferent to the remonstrances of the Marquis of Botta, Austrian ambassador to St. Petersburg. According to that diplomat, a fine specialist in public and private affairs, the regent's lover was making a mistake to persevere in an adulterous liaison that was likely to turn against him several of the high-ranking persons in Russia and in his own government in Saxony. He suggested a cynical and adroit solution that would satisfy everyone.

Being widowed, unencumbered and pleasant-looking, why shouldn't Lynar ask for the hand of Julie Mengden, Anna Leopoldovna's beloved? Satisfying the two of them (one legitimately, the second clandestinely), he would make them both happy and nobody could reproach him for leading the regent to sin. Lynar found the idea appealing; he promised to consider it. What encouraged him to go ahead was that, contrary to what he might have feared, Anna Leopoldovna — duly consulted — did not see any harm in this charming combination. She even thought that, by becoming Lynar's wife, Julie Mengden would strengthen the loving union between three beings that God, in his subtle clairvoyance, had chosen to make inseparable.

However, the practical application of the arrangement was delayed to enable Lynar to go to Germany, where he intended to settle some urgent family matters. Actually, he took out a large quantity of precious stones in his baggage, the sale of which would be used to build up a "war chest" in case the regent should think of having herself proclaimed empress. During his absence, Anna Leopoldovna exchanged an encrypted correspondence with him, using the pretext to swear their reciprocal love and to determine what role the future countess of Lynar would play in the trio. Above each line, the regent's letters contain various annotations indicating the true meaning of the message, duly transcribed by a secretary. "As regards Juliette [Julie Mengden], how can you doubt her [my] love and her [my] fondness, after all the signs that I have given you. If you like her [me], do not go on with such reproaches, if her [my] health is of any concern to you. . . . Let me know when you are coming back, and enjoy the certainty that you have all of my affection, [I kiss you and I am very much yours] Anna."[1]

Separated from Lynar, Anna Leopoldovna found it more and more difficult to put up with her husband's reproaches. Nevertheless, needing comfort in the desert of her solitude, she allowed him to visit her in bed from time to time. But he would have to be satisfied with that — just an interim, before the return of the regent's authentic bed-partner. The Prussian minister, Axel of Mardefeld, observer of the morals of the court of Russia, wrote to his sovereign on October 17, 1741, "She [the regent] has entrusted all matters to [her husband, Anthony Ulrich] so that she can devote her time more freely to leisure and entertainment, which renders him necessary, in a way. It remains to be seen whether she will rely on him the same way when she has a declared favorite. Basically, she does not love him; thus he has had permission to sleep with her only since the departure of Narcissus [Lynar]."[2]

While she was struggling in this sentimental imbroglio, the men around her were only thinking about politics. After Bühren's downfall, Münnich was given the title of Prime Minister, a reward of 170,000 rubles for services rendered, and the rank of second man in the empire after Anthony Ulrich, father of the child tsar. However, this avalanche of benefices began to irritate Anthony Ulrich. He found that his wife had exaggerated in the display of gratitude towards a servant of the State who was very effective, certainly, but lowly of birth. He was joined in his criticism by other figures whose sensibilities had been wounded by this distribution of emoluments. Among those who felt they had been overlooked by those in power were Loewenwolde, Ostermann, and Mikhail Golovkin. They complained that they were being treated like subalterns, when in fact the regent and her husband were deeply indebted to them.

Obviously, the all-powerful Münnich was at the head of this gang. However, the field marshal suddenly took ill, and had to be confined to bed. Taking advantage of this timely indisposition, Ostermann was quick to move in, seeking to take over various portfolios and shunt aside his principal rival, giving orders in his stead. Barely out of sickbed, Münnich tried to take control again — but it was too late. Ostermann was well-entrenched. He was not about to let go of anything, and Anna Leopoldovna, advised by Julie Mengden, decided that the moment had come for her to assert all her rights, with Ostermann standing behind her like a guardian angel. He proposed looking for international backing and even subsidies to support a "cleansing of the monarchy." Confused negotiations were initiated in St. Petersburg with England, Austria, and Saxony for alliances that would go nowhere. But let's admit it: nobody among the European diplomats had faith in Russia any more, caught as it was in cross currents. The ship had no captain. Even in Constantinople, an unforeseen collusion between France and Turkey hinted at the possible recrudescence of bellicose inclinations.

Although they had been kept ignorant of developments in the sphere of foreign relations, the army officers suffered nonetheless from their fatherland's obliteration and even humiliation, in international confrontations. The insolence and the whims of the Count of Lynar, who allowed himself every license since his marriage with Julie Mengden was concocted in the back rooms of the palace, finished off any little sympathy the regent might have preserved among the people and the middle nobility. The *gvardeitsy* (the men of the imperial guard) reproached her for scorning the military, and her humblest subjects were astonished that she was never seen walking freely about the city as all the other tsarinas had done. She was said to dislike the barracks as much as the street, and that she only had time for the salons. She was also said to have such an appetite for pleasure that she never bothered to fasten her clothes unless she was attending a reception; that way, she could get out of them more quickly when her lover came to visit her.

On the other hand, her aunt Elizabeth Petrovna, although

most of the time confined in a kind of semi-voluntary, semi-imposed exile far from the capital, had more taste for human interactions, simple and direct relations, and even reached out to the masses. Taking full advantage of her rare visits to St. Petersburg, this true daughter of Peter the Great was quick to show herself in public, traveling about on horseback or in an open carriage in the city; and she would respond to the public's greetings with a gracious wave of the hand and an angelic smile. Her approach was so natural that, when she was passing by, everyone felt authorized to shout out his joy or his sorrow to her, as if she were a sister of charity. It was said that soldiers on leave would go up to the sides of her sleigh to murmur a compliment in her ear. Among themselves, they called her *Matushka*, "little mother"; she knew that, and was proud to consider it an additional title of nobility.

One of the first to have detected the tsarevna's discreetly rising star among the ordinary people and the middle aristocracy was the French ambassador, the marquis de La Chétardie. He very quickly understood the advantages he could derive for his country and himself by winning Elizabeth Petrovna's confidence, and even friendship.

He was assisted in this campaign of diplomatic seduction by the princess's designated doctor, a Hanoverian of French origin, Armand Lestocq, whose ancestors had settled in Germany after the Revocation of the Edict of Nantes. This man, about 50 years old, skilled in his art and absolutely amoral in his private conduct, had been introduced to Elizabeth Petrovna when she was only an obscure young girl, flirtatious and sensual. The marquis de La Chétardie often called upon him to try to penetrate the tsarevna's varying moods and the shifting public opinion in Russia. What stood out, in Lestocq's comments, was that unlike the women who had preceded her at the head of the country, this one found France very attractive. She had learned French and even "danced the minuet" in her childhood. Although she read very little, she appreciated the spirit of that nation that was supposed to be courageous, and at the same time, rebellious and frivolous. She surely could get over the fact that, in her early youth, she had been offered in marriage to Louis XV, before being offered (without any greater success), to the prince-bishop of Lübeck and finally to Peter II, who had died prematurely. The mirage of Versailles continued to dazzle her, despite the many disappointments in love that she had suffered. Those who admired her grace and her expansive exuberance, as she entered her thirtieth year, claimed that in spite of her plumpness she "made men hot," that she her skirt was very light and that, in her vicinity, one had the sensation of being surrounded by French music. The Saxon agent Lefort wrote, with a mixture of respect and impertinence, "It seems that she was, indeed, born for France, as she likes only superficial glitter."[3] For his part, the English ambassador Edward Finch, while recognizing that the tsarevna was very spirited, judged her "too fat to conspire."[4]

However, Elizabeth Petrovna's penchant for the French refinements of fashion and culture did not keep her from reveling in Russian rusticity when it came to her nightly pleasures. Even before she held an official position at her niece's court, she took as her lover a Ukrainian peasant who had been named cantor in the choir of the palace chapel: Alexis Razumovsky. His deep voice, athletic physique and crude ways were all the more appreciated in the bedroom, coming as they did after hours spent amid the affectations and the mincing ways of the salons. An avid consumer of simple carnal satisfactions and elegance as well, the princess expressed her true nature through this contradiction. A full-blooded man, Alexis Razumovsky had a weakness for drink, often for too much drink, and when he had had his fill he would sometimes raise his voice, utter coarse words, and toss about the furniture, while his mistress was a little bit frightened and very much amused by his vulgarity. Hearing about this "misalliance," those fastidious advisers who were in close communication with the tsarevna recommended she conduct herself with prudence, or at least discretion, in order to avoid a damaging scandal. However, both the Shuvalovs (Alexander and Ivan), the chamberlain Mikhail Vorontsov and most of Elizabeth's partisans had to admit that, in the barracks and on the street, the news of this liaison between the daughter of Peter the Great and a man of the people was greeted with indulgence and even good-naturedness — as if the folks "at the bottom" liked her all the more for not scorning one of their own.

At the same time, in the palace, the Francophile party was getting cozier with Elizabeth. That rendered her suspicious to Ostermann who, as a declared champion of the Germanic cause in Russia, was unlikely to tolerate the least obstacle to his plans. When the British ambassador Edward Finch asked his opinion of the princess's overt preferences in international relations, he peevishly retorted that, if she continued to exhibit such "ambiguous conduct," she would be "locked up in a convent." Reporting this conversation in one of his dispatches, the Englishman observed ironically: "That could be a dangerous expedient, for she is not at all suited to the life of a nun and she is extremely popular."[5]

He was right. From one day to the next, dissatisfaction was escalating within the regiments of the Guard. The men secretly wondered what they were waiting for, in the palace, to drive out all the Germans who were lording it over the Russian. From the humblest of the *gvardeitsy* to the highest officers, they decried the injustice done to the daughter of Peter the Great, sole heiress of the Romanov line and lineage, by depriving her of the crown. Some dared to insinuate that the regent, her outsider of a husband Anthony Ulrich and her baby of a tsar were all usurpers. Contrast

to that lot the luminous goodness of the *matushka* Elizabeth Petrovna, who, as they said, showed "the spark of Peter the Great."
Already, seditious cries could be heard in the city outskirts. In the
depths of their barracks, the soldiers muttered among themselves,
after an exhausting and pointless review, "Isn't there anyone who
can order us to take up our weapons in favor of the *matushka*?"[6]

Despite the frequency of these spontaneous demonstrations,
the marquis de La Chétardie still hesitated to promise France's
moral support for a coup d'état. But Lestocq, supported by
Schwartz (a former German captain who had gone over into the
service of Russia), decided that the moment had come to acquaint
the army with the plot. However, at the same time, the Swedish
minister Nolken let La Chétardie know that his government had
given him a credit line of 100,000 ecus to help consolidate Anna
Leopoldovna's hold on power, or, "according to the circumstances," to bolster the aspirations of the tsarevna Elizabeth Petrovna. It was his call. Put in an awkward position by a decision
that was beyond his competence to make, Nolken relied on his
French colleague for guidance. La Chétardie, a prudent man, was
terrified by such a responsibility and, no more able to make up his
mind than Nolken had been, answered evasively. On this subject,
Paris urged him to go along with Sweden and to quietly support
the cause of Elizabeth Petrovna.

Having been brought up to date on these unexpected devel-
opments, it was Elizabeth's turn to hesitate. Should she take the
plunge? She could already see what would happen if she failed —
she would be denounced, thrown into prison, have her head
shaved, and end her days in a loneliness worse than death. La
Chétardie shared a similar concern for himself and admitted that
he no longer closed his eyes at night, and that at the least noise he
would "run to the window, believing that all was lost."[7] And furthermore, he had already incurred the wrath of Ostermann, re-

cently, following an alleged diplomatic *faux pas*; he had been invited not to set foot again in the Summer Palace until further orders. He took refuge in the villa that he had let at the gates of the capital, but he did not feel safe anywhere. He took to receiving Elizabeth's emissaries on the sly, preferably at nightfall. He believed he had been politically excommunicated, for good; but, after a period of penitence, Ostermann authorized him to tender his letters of accreditation — provided that he presented them to the baby tsar in person. Once again admitted to the court, the ambassador took the opportunity to meet Elizabeth Petrovna and to murmur to her, during an aside, that France had great plans for her. Serene and smiling, she replied, "Being the daughter of Peter the Great, I believe I remain faithful to my father's memory by placing my confidence in the friendship of France and in asking for its support in exercising my proper rights."[8]

La Chétardie was careful not to reveal these subversive remarks, but the rumor of a conspiracy began to spread throughout the regent's entourage. At once, Anna Leopoldovna's supporters were aflame with vindicatory zeal. Anthony Ulrich, as her husband, and the count of Lynar, as her favorite, both warned her of the risk she was running. They urged her to increase the security at the gates of the imperial residence and to arrest the ambassador of France at once. Impassive, she shrugged off these rumors and refused to overreact. She doubted her informants' reports; but her chief rival, Elizabeth, having heard of the suspicions that swirled around her undertaking, was alarmed and begged La Chétardie to take greater care. Bundles of compromising documents were burned and Elizabeth, out of prudence, left the capital. She found some early conspirators in friendly villas close to Peterhof.

On August 13, 1741, Russia went to war with Sweden. The diplomats may have known the obscure reasons behind this conflict, but the people did not. All that was known, in the countryside, was that on the grounds of some very convoluted questions of national prestige, borders, and the succession, thousands of men were going to die, far from home, at the hand of the enemy. But, for the moment, the imperial guard was not involved. And that was all.

At the end of November 1741, Elizabeth sadly noted that a plot as adventurous as hers would go nowhere without solid financial backing. Called to the rescue, La Chétardie scraped up what funds he could, and then called for the court of France to extend an additional advance of 15,000 ducats. As the French government persisted in turning a deaf ear, Lestocq prodded La Chétardie to take action, come what may, without waiting for Paris or Versailles to give him the go-ahead. Pressured, pushed, and with Lestocq twisting his arm, the ambassador went to the tsarevna and, painting a darker than necessary picture, asserted that according to the latest information the regent was preparing to have her thrown into a convent. Lestocq, who was there to back him up, confirmed without so much as raising a brow that she might be taken away and imprisoned any day. Such an eventuality was, indeed, precisely the nightmare that tormented Elizabeth. To convince her fully, Lestocq (who had some artistic talent) took a scrap of paper and made two sketches: in one, a sovereign was taking her throne, acclaimed by all the people, and in the other the same woman was taking the veil and walking, head bowed, toward a convent. He placed the two drawings under Elizabeth's nose and barked:

"Choose, Madam!"

"Very well," the tsarevna answered; "I leave it to you to determine the moment!"[9]

She did not say anything, but one could read her fear in her eyes. Without regard for her pallor and her quaking nerves, Lestocq and La Chétardie drew up a detailed list of all her adversaries who would have to be arrested as soon as the victory was hers; at the top of the list, of course, was Ostermann. But there was also Ernst Münnich, son of the field marshal; Baron Mengden, father of Julie, so dear to the heart of the regent; Count Golovkin, Loewenwolde and some of their associates. However, they did not yet pronounce themselves on the fate that awaited, in the final analysis, the regent, her husband, her lover and her baby. Everything in its own time! To urge on the tsarevna, who was too timid for his liking, Lestocq affirmed that the soldiers of the Guard were ready to defend, through her, "the blood of Peter the Great." At these words, she suddenly took heart and, galvanized, dazed, declared: "I will not betray that blood!"

This secret, decisive meeting took place in great secrecy on November 22, 1741. The following day, a reception was held at the palace. Hiding her anxiety, Elizabeth presented herself at the court wearing a ceremonial gown calculated to pique all her rivals and a smile calculated to disarm the most malevolent spirits. Greeting the regent, she was apprehensive that she might hear some affront or an allusion to her friendships with gentlemen of not very suitable opinions, but Anna Leopoldovna seemed even more gracious than usual. She must have been too preoccupied with her love for the count of Lynar (who was away on a journey), and her fondness for Julie Mengden (whose wedding trousseau she was preparing), and the health of her son (whom she was coddling "like a good German mother," as they said), to let herself get carried away with the endless rumors that were circulating about an alleged plot.

However, taking another look at her aunt, the tsarevna, so beautiful and so serene, she recalled that in his last letter Lynar had warned her that La Chétardie and Lestocq were playing a double game and that, impelled by France and perhaps even by Sweden, they seemed to have in mind overthrowing her in favor of

Elizabeth Petrovna. Suddenly shaken, Anna Leopoldovna decided to clear the air. Seeing that her aunt was seated nearby, playing cards with some of the courtiers, she walked over, drew her aside, and asked her to follow her to a private room. Once alone with her, she spelled out the accusation that she had so recently heard. Elizabeth was thunderstruck — she blenched, panicked, protested her innocence, swore that Anna had been misinformed, odiously misled — and threw herself at her niece's feet, in tears. Anna, upset by Elizabeth's apparent sincerity, burst into tears, herself. Thus, instead of clashing, the two women embraced each other in a mingling of sighs and promises of good feelings. By the end of the evening, they parted like two sisters who had been brought closer by a shared danger.

But, as soon as the incident became known among their supporters, it took on the significance of a call to action. A few hours later, dining in a famous restaurant where oysters from Holland were sold as well as wigs from Paris, and which was moreover a meeting place for some of the best-informed men in the capital, Lestocq learned, via well-placed informers, that Ostermann had given orders for the Preobrazhensky Regiment (which was entirely behind the tsarevna) to move away from St. Petersburg. The pretext for this abrupt troop movement was the unexpected outbreak of war between Sweden and Russia; actually, it was as good a means as any other to deprive Elizabeth Petrovna of her surest allies in the event of a coup d'état.

The die was cast. They had better move quickly. Ignoring protocol, an impromptu meeting was held clandestinely, right in the palace, in the tsarevna's apartments. The principal conspirators were all there, surrounding Elizabeth Petrovna, who was more dead than alive. At her side, Alexis Razumovsky gave his opinion on the question, for the first time. Summarizing the general opinion, he declared in his beautiful, deep voice, "If we drag our feet now, we will only bring about a great misfortune. I feel it in my soul — we are on the verge of great chaos, destruction, perhaps even the ruin of the fatherland!" La Chétardie and Lestocq agreed, vociferously. There was no way out, now. Her back to the wall, Elizabeth Petrovna sighed and reluctantly acquiesced: "Alright, since if you push me to do it." And, not even completing her sentence, she made vague gesture and left it to fate to decide the rest.

Without a moment's hesitation, now, Lestocq and La Chétardie assigned roles; Her Highness would have to go to the *gvardeitsy* in person to enlist them in her aid. And just then, a delegation of grenadiers from the Guard, led by Sergeant Grünstein, had just turned up at the Summer Palace to request an audience with the tsarevna: these men confirmed that they, too, had just received orders to leave for the Finnish border. *In extremis*, the insurrectionists were condemned to succeed. Every minute lost would decrease their chances. Faced with the most crucial decision in her life, Elizabeth withdrew to her own room.

Before jumping into the breach, she knelt down before the icons and swore to revoke the death penalty all across Russia, should they succeed in their enterprise. In the next room her partisans, gathered around Alexis Razumovsky, fretted over these delays. She wasn't going to change her mind again, was she? At the end of his patience, La Chétardie returned to his embassy.

When Elizabeth reappeared, standing tall, radiant and proud, Armand Lestocq placed a cross of silver in her hands, pronounced a few more words of encouragement, draped around her neck the cord of the Order of Saint Catherine, and pushed her out the door. A sleigh was waiting. Elizabeth took her seat, with Lestocq; Razumovsky and Saltykov settled into a second sleigh, while Vorontsov and Shuvalov rode along on horseback. Behind them came Grünstein and ten grenadiers. The entire group set out, in the night, toward the barracks of the Preobrazhensky Regiment. They halted briefly in front of the French embassy, where Elizabeth sought to inform her "accomplice" La Chétardie that the dénouement was at hand; but a secretary affirmed that His Excellency was not in. Understanding that this absence was essentially diplomatic, intended to clear the ambassador in case of failure, the tsarevna did not insist. She merely relayed the message, via an embassy attaché, that she was "dashing to glory under the aegis of France." And to her merit she affirmed, loud and clear, that the French government had just refused her the 2,000 rubles that she had asked for, as a last resort, from La Chétardie.

Arriving at the barracks, the plotters ran into a sentinel whom no one had had time to forewarn; doing his duty, he pounded out an alarm on his drum. Quick as lightning, Lestocq slashed the drum with his sword, while Grünstein's grenadiers hurried to inform their comrades of the patriotic act that was expected of them. The officers, who lodged in the city, nearby, were also alerted. Within minutes, several hundred men formed up, ready for action. Gathering her courage, Elizabeth stepped down from the sleigh and addressed them in a tone of affectionate command. She had prepared her speech well.

"Do you recognize me? Do you know whose daughter I am?"

"*Da, matushka!*" the soldiers answered in unison.

"They plan to send me to a monastery. Will you follow me, to prevent that?"

"We are ready, *matushka!* We will kill them all!"

"If you speak of killing, I must withdraw! I do not want anyone killed!"

This magnanimous answer disconcerted the *gvardeitsy*. How could anyone ask them to fight, while sparing the enemy? Was the tsarevna less sure of her rights than they had thought? Understanding that she had disappointed them with her tolerance, she held up the silver cross that she had received from Lestocq and exclaimed: "I swear to die for you! Swear to do as much for me, but without spilling any blood unnecessarily!" That was a promise the *gvardeitsy* could give without reserve. They swore their fealty in a thunder of enthusiasm and advanced, in turn, to kiss the cross that she held out to them like the priests do in church. Seeing that the final obstacle had just come down, Elizabeth embraced with her gaze the regiment lined up before her, its officers and its men, took a deep breath and declares in a prophetic voice: "Let us go forth and bring joy to our fatherland!" Then she mounted the sleigh once more and the horses sprang forward.

Three hundred silent men followed the *matushka* along the still-deserted Nevsky Prospect, heading for the Winter Palace. Passing by the Admiralty, she thought that the great sound of marching feet and the neighing of the horses must surely catch the attention of a sentinel or some townsman who suffered from in-somnia. Descending from her sleigh, she thought of making it the rest of the way on foot. But her ankle boots sank deep in the snow. She faltered. Two grenadiers dashed forward to help, picked her up in their arms and carried her all the way to the en-trance of the palace. Having arrived at the guard post, eight men from the escort, detached by Lestocq, advanced with grim faces and gave the password that had been communicated to them by an accomplice, disarming the four sentries planted in front of the gate. The officer who commanded the guard shouted, "*Na Karaul!* ("To arms!"). One of the grenadiers pointed his bayonet at the fellow's chest, ready to slit him open at the first sign of resistance. But Elizabeth set aside the weapon with a sweep of her hand. This gesture of leniency completely won over the detachment charged with ensuring palace security.

Meanwhile, a few of the conspirators had reached the "private apartments." Coming to the regent's room, Elizabeth surprised her in bed. Her lover still being away, Anna Leopoldovna was sleeping beside her husband. She opened her frightened eyes to find the tsarevna staring down at her with a disconcerting gentleness. Without raising her voice, Elizabeth said to her, "It's time to get up, little sister!" Stupefied, the regent did not move. But Anthony Ulrich, having awakened in his turn, protested loudly and called for the Guard with all his might. Nobody came running. While he continued to holler, Anna Leopoldovna was first to realize that she had been defeated; she accepted this with the docility of a sleepwalker, and only asked that she not be separated from Julie Mengden.

While the couple self-consciously dressed, under the suspicious eye of the conspirators, Elizabeth went into the child's room. There lay the baby tsar, resting in his cradle all draped with voile and lace. A moment later, disturbed by the commotion, he opened his eyes and let out an inarticulate wail. Leaning over him, Elizabeth cooed with feigned affection — or was she truly touched? Then she picked up the infant in her arms, took it over toward the guards (all melting at this tender sight), and said in a tone that was distinct enough to be heard by one and all, "Poor little dear, you are innocent! Your parents alone are guilty!"

As a seasoned actress, she did not need the applause of her public to know that she had just scored another point. Having pronounced this sentence, which she (rightly) judged historical, she carried off the child in his diapers, robbing the cradle, and mounted once again her sleigh, still holding little Ivan VI in her arms. The first light of dawn was just gracing the city; the weather was very cold. The sky was heavy with fog and snow. Some rare early risers, having caught wind of great events, ran to see the tsarevna drive by; they howled out a hoarse hurrah.

This was the fifth coup d'état in fifteen years in their good city, all with the support of the Guard. They had become so accustomed to these sudden shifts of the political wind that they did not even speculate anymore as to who was actually running the country, among all these high-ranking persons whose names were honored one day and drawn through the mud the next.

Awakening to hear the news of this latest upheaval in the imperial palace *cum* theatre, the Scottish general Lascy, who had long been in the service of Russia, did not show any hint of surprise. When his interlocutor, curious to know his preferences, asked him, "Whom are you for?" he philosophically retorted, "For the one who reigns!" On the morning of November 25, 1741, this response might have spoken for all the Russians, except those who lost their positions or their fortunes due to the change.[10]

Footnotes

1. Letter dated 13 October 1741, published by Soloviev, *Histoire de Russie*, and cited by K. Waliszewski, *op. cit.*
2. K. Waliszewski, *Ibid.*
3. Cf. Mirnievitch: *La Femme russe au XVIII siècle*, and Waliszewski, *op. cit.*
4. *Ibid.*
5. Cited by Daria Olivier, *op. cit.*
6. Cf. Soloviev, *op. cit.*
7. Letter from La Chétardie to his minister, Amelot de Chailloux, dated 30 May (10 June) 1741; cf. Waliszewski, *op. cit.*
8. *Ibid.*
9. Cf. Miliukov, Seignobos and Eisenmann, *Histoire de Russie.*
10. Elizabeth's coup d'état and the remarks made at the time were reported in numerous documents dating from that period, including *Les Archives du prince M. L. Vorontsov*, and collected by K. Waliszewski, in *L'Héritage de Pierre le Grand.*

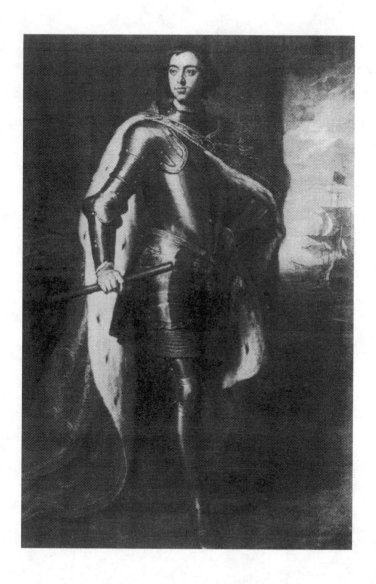

Peter the Great, by G. Kneller. London, Kensington Palace.
Photo A. C. Cooper (copyright reserved).

St. Petersburg in the time of Peter the Great.
The Neva Embankment, the Admiralty, and the Academy of Sciences.
Bibliothèque nationale de France, Prints Division. Photo B.N.

View of the Isaakievsky Bridge and St. Isaac's Cathedral, the Winter Palace,
and the Hermitage, in St. Petersburg.
Photo Giraudon.

The Winter Palace, St. Petersburg, 1843.
Russian School, Sodovnikov.
Preserved in Peterhof Library. Photo Josse.

The grand palace and the park at Tsarskoye Selo.
Engraving by Damane-Demartrais.

Catherine I (1682-1727), wife of Peter I (The Great).
Empress of Russia (1725-1727).

Empress Anna Ivanovna on her coronation day (1730).
After an engraving printed in Moscow.

Portrait of Elizabeth Petrovna, Empress of Russia (1741-1762), daughter of Peter the Great.
Copper engraving, 1761, by Georg Friedrich Schmidt (1696-1772), after a 1758 painting by Louis Toque (1696-1772).

Elizabeth 1st (1709-1762) on the anniversary of her coronation day.
The soldiers swear their fidelity to her. Russian School (1883).
St. Petersburg, The Hermitage Museum. Photo Josse.

Elizabeth Petrovna, Empress of Russia (1741-1761).
"Tsarina Elizabeth Petrovna, Portrait on horseback, with a Moor."
Painted in 1743 by Georg Christoph Grooth (1716-1749). Detail.
Painted on canvas, 85 x 68.3 cm.
Moscow, Tretyakov Gallery.

Catherine II the Great (1729-1796) in her coronation gown.
By Stefano Torelli (1712-1784),
Italian School.
St. Petersburg, The Hermitage
Museum. Photo Josse.

Catherine II the Great. Empress of
Russia (1729-1796).
"The Coronation of Catherine II."
Painted in 1777 by Stefano Torelli.
Oil on canvas. Moscow. AKG Photo.

VII

ELIZABETH'S TRIUMPH

Coups d'état having become a political tradition in Russia, Elizabeth felt morally and historically obliged to follow the protocol that usually applied in such extreme moments: solemnly proclaiming one's rights to the throne, arresting one's opponents *en masse*, and showering rewards upon one's supporters. She must not have slept more than two hours that agitated night — but in moments of euphoria, the thrill of success is more reinvigorating than a simple nap could ever be. She was up at the break of day, beautifully dressed and beautifully coifed, smiling as if she had just enjoyed a refreshing sleep. Twenty courtiers were already squeezing themselves into her antechamber, seeking to be the first to pay homage to the new ruler. In a glance she discerned which of them were genuinely delighted by her victory and which were merely prostrating themselves before her in the hope of avoiding the punishment that they deserved. Deferring the pleasure of acting upon that judgment, she showed a pleasant face to all and, waving them aside, stepped out onto the balcony.

Below stood the regiments who had come to swear their allegiance to her. The soldiers, in parade formation, howled with joy — without breaking ranks. Their eyes shone as savagely as their bayonets. To Elizabeth, the cheers shattering the icy early morning air were an eloquent declaration of love to the "little mother." Behind this rampart of gray uniforms, the people of St. Petersburg crowded together, as impatient as the army to express its surprise and its approval. Facing this unanimous joy, it was very tempting for a sensitive woman to forgive those who had misplaced their loyalties. But Elizabeth stiffened her resolve against an indulgence that she might come to regret later on. She knew, through atavism if not through personal experience, that authority precludes charity. With a cold-minded wisdom, she chose to savor her happiness without giving up her resentment.

To avoid any confusion, she dispatched Prince Nikita Trubetskoy to bring the various embassies the official news of Her Majesty Elizabeth I's accession to the throne; most of the foreign ministers had already been apprised of this event. No doubt the most pleased was His Excellency Jacques-Joachim Trotti de La Chétardie, who had made this cause his personal mission. Elizabeth's triumph was to some extent his triumph, and he hoped to be suitably rewarded both by the principal interested party and by the French government.

He went by barouche to the Winter Palace to greet the new tsarina; along the way, the grenadiers who had taken part in the heroic tumult of the day before, and who were still wandering about in the streets, recognized him as he went by and gave him a formal escort, calling him *batiushka frantsuz* ("our French papa") and "Guardian of Peter the Great's daughter." La Chétardie was moved to tears by this touching warmth. Seeing that the Russians had more heart than the French, and not wishing to let them down, he invited all these brave military men to come and drink to the health of France and Russia on the embassy grounds. However, when he related this little anecdote to his minister, Amelot de Chailloux, the latter reproached him sharply: "These compliments from the grenadiers, which you unfortunately could not avoid, have exposed the role you played in the revolution,"[1] he wrote to him on January 15, 1741.

In the meanwhile, Elizabeth had ordered a *Te Deum* and a special religious service to underscore the troops' oath of loyalty. She also took care to publish a proclamation justifying her accession "under the terms of our legitimate right and because of our blood proximity to our dear father and our dear mother, the Emperor Peter the Great and the Empress Catherine Alexeyevna; and also in accordance with the unanimous and so humble request of those who have been faithful to us."[2]

The reprisals announced in tandem with all this celebration were severe. The secondary players in the counter-conspiracy joined the principal "instigators" (Münnich, Loewenwolde, Ostermann and Golovkin) in the cells of the Peter and Paul Fortress. Prince Nikita Trubetskoy, charged with judging the culprits, wasted no time with pointless formalities. Magistrates were named on the spur of the moment to assist him in his deliberations, and all their sentences were final. A large crowd of spectators, eager to applaud the misfortunes of others, followed the sessions hour by hour. There were many foreigners among the accused, which delighted "the good Russians." Some of these vengeful spirits took particular pleasure in stating, with a laugh, that in this it was Russia suing Germany. Elizabeth is said to have sat behind a curtain, listening to every word of the proceedings. In any case, the verdicts were largely (or entirely) dictated by her.

Most of the defendants were sentenced to death. Of course,

during the coup d'état just the day before, she had sworn she would end capital punishment in Russia; therefore, Her Majesty allowed herself the innocent pleasure of granting clemency at the last minute. She considered that such sadism tinged with leniency was part of her ancestral instinct, since Peter the Great had had a record of mixing cruelty and lucidity, entertainment and horror. However, each time the court chaired by Nikita Trubetskoy issued a death penalty, it had to specify the means of execution. Trubetskoy's men were most often satisfied with decapitation by axe; but when it came to deciding Ostermann's fate, voices in the crowd protested that such humanity would be out of place. At the request of Vasily Dolgoruky, who had just been retrieved from exile and who was frothing with a desire for revenge, Ostermann was condemned to be tortured on the wheel before being beheaded; Münnich was to be drawn and quartered before the death-blow was delivered. Only the most humdrum criminals would be spared torture and arrive before the executioner intact.

Until the very day and hour that had been set for the execution, Elizabeth kept her compassionate intentions secret. The hour had arrived. The culprits were dragged to the scaffold before a crowd that was baying for the "traitors'" blood. Suddenly, a messenger from the palace brought word that, in her infinite kindness, Her Majesty had deigned to commute their sentences to exile in perpetuity. The spectators, at first disappointed at being deprived of such an amusing spectacle, wanted to attack the beneficiaries of this imperial favor; then, as though suddenly enlightened, they blessed their *matushka* who had showed herself to be a better Christian than they were by thus sparing the lives of the "infamous perpetrators." Impressed by her clemency, some ventured to suggest that this exceptional restraint was due to the deeply feminine nature of Her Majesty and that a tsar, in her place, would have shown far greater rigor in expressing his wrath. They even proposed that Russia would be better off in the future if it were always ruled by a woman. In their opinion the people, in their misery, were more in need of a mother than a father.

While everyone was celebrating the fact that these big political criminals had finally been brought down, and praising the tsarina for her heart of gold, Münnich was shipped off to end his days in Pelym, a Siberian village 3000 versts from St. Petersburg; Loewenwolde died in Solikamsk, Ostermann in Berezov, in the Tobolsk region, and Golovkin — well, exactly where he was to be sent was not clearly indicated on the passenger waybill, so he was simply ditched in some Siberian village along the way. The members of the Brunswick family, with the ex-regent Anna Leopoldovna at their head, received better treatment because of their high birth; they were consigned to Riga, before being dispatched to Kholmogory, in the far north.

Having eliminated her adversaries, Elizabeth now had to hurry to replace those experienced men whose removal had left key positions vacant. Lestocq and Vorontsov were the chief recruiters. They invited Alexis Petrovich Bestuzhev to succeed Ostermann, and his brother, Mikhail Bestuzhev, replaced Loewenwolde as Master of the Royal Hunt. Among the military men, the most brilliant promotion was granted to Dolgoruky, newly returned from exile. Even subordinates (the most conscientious of them) did well during this period when reparations were being made for the injustices of the preceding reign. The new beneficiaries of imperial largesse shared the spoils taken from those who had lost. Commenting on this waltz, Mardefeld wrote to Frederick II: "Count Loewenwolde's clothing, underwear, hose and linens were distributed among the empress's chamberlains, who were naked as a hand. Of the four most recently named gentlemen of the chamber, two had been lackeys and a third had served as stableman."[3]

As for the leading protagonists, Elizabeth rewarded them far more than they could have hoped. Lestocq became a count, private counselor to Her Majesty, premier doctor to the court, and director of "the college of medicine" with a 7,000-ruble annual retainer for life. Mikhail Vorontsov, Alexander Shuvalov and Alexis Razumovsky awoke the next day (and a beautiful morning it was) as grand chamberlains and knights of St. Andrew. At the same time, the entire company of grenadiers of the Preobrazhensky Regiment, which had contributed to the tsarina's success on November 25, 1741, was converted into a company of personal bodyguards for Her Majesty under the Germanic name of the *Leib-Kompania*. Every man and every officer of this elite unit was promoted one level; their uniforms were adorned with an escutcheon bearing the device "Fidelity and Zeal." Some were even brought into the nobility, with hereditary titles, together with gifts of lands and up to 2,000 rubles. Alexis Razumovsky and Mikhail Vorontsov, who had no military knowledge whatsoever, were named Lieutenant Generals, with concomitant rewards of money and domains.

Despite all this repeated generosity, the leaders of the coup d'état were always asking for more. Far from appeasing them, the tsarina's prodigality turned their heads. They thought she "owed them everything" because they had "given their all." Their worship for the *matushka* devolved into familiarity, even impertinence. Within Elizabeth's entourage, the men of the *Leib-Kompania* were called the "creative grenadiers," since they had "created" the new sovereign, or "Her Majesty's big kids," since she treated them with an almost maternal indulgence. Aggravated by the insolence of these low class parvenus, Mardefeld complained in a dispatch to King Frederick II of Prussia, "They [the empress's grenadiers] refuse to get out of the court, they are well-entrenched, . . . they walk in the galleries where Her Majesty holds her court, they mingle with people of the first quality, . . . they stuff their faces at the same table where the empress sits, and she is so nice to them that she has gone as far as to sign an order to print the image of a grenadier on the back of the new rubles."[4]

In a report dating from the same month and year Edward Finch, the English ambassador, wrote that the bodyguards assigned to the palace had deserted their stations one fine day in order to protest the disciplinary action inflicted upon one of them by their superior officer, the Prince of Hesse-Homburg; Her Majesty was indignant that anyone should have dared to punish her "children" without asking her authorization and she embraced the victims of such iniquity.

She always tried to give preference to Russians when making appointments to sensitive positions, but she was often forced to call upon foreigners to fulfill functions requiring a minimum of competence, despite her good intentions. Thus, given the lack of qualified personnel, one after another of Münnich's former victims reappeared in St. Petersburg to populate the ministries and chancelleries. Devier and Brevern, back in the saddle, brought in other Germans including Siewers and Flück.

To justify these inevitable offenses to Slavic nationalism, Elizabeth cited her model Peter the Great who, in his own words, had wanted to "open a window on Europe." France was, certainly, at the center of this ideal Europe, with its light take on life, its fine culture and philosophical irony; but there was Germany, too — such a thoughtful, disciplined, industrious nation, so rich in military and commercial professionals, so well-endowed with princes and princesses in need of marriage partners! Could Elizabeth fish, according to her needs, in both of these ponds? Should she really refrain from employing experienced men, simply in order to Russianize everything? Her dream would be to reconcile the local customs with new ideas from abroad, to enrich the ways of the Russophiles, so much in love with their past, by bringing in contributions from the West, to create a German or French Russia without betraying the traditions of the fatherland.

While pondering which way to turn, under pressure from the Marquis de La Chétardie (pleading in favor of France), Mardefeld (promoting Germany's interests), and Bestuzhev (a resolute Russian traditionalist), she had to decide on domestic policies of every sort, questions that seemed to her to be of great importance as well. She therefore reorganized the old Senate so that it would wield the legislature and the judiciary powers from that point forward; she replaced the dysfunctional Cabinet with Her Majesty's private Chancellery, and she increased various fines; she raised the *octroi* taxes and encouraged settlement by foreign colonists to populate the uninhabited regions of southern Russia. But these strictly administrative measures did not ease her main worry. How could she ensure the future of the dynasty? What would become of the country if, for one reason or another, she had to "pass on the torch"?

Since she did not have a child of her own, she was deeply afraid that after she died — or as a result of some conspiracy — the young ex-tsar Ivan VI, now dethroned, would succeed her. For the moment, the baby and his parents were safely tucked away in Riga. But they were liable to come back into favor some day, through one of those political upheavals that had become so common in Russia. To preclude any such possibility, Elizabeth could only think of one possible course of action: she would have to name an heir now, and have him be accepted. However, the candidates were few and the choice seemed apparent: the only appropriate recipient of this supreme burden was the son of her deceased sister Anna Petrovna, the young prince Charles Peter Ulrich of Holstein-Gottorp.

The boy's father, Charles Frederick of Holstein-Gottorp, had died in 1739; now the orphan, who was about 14 years old, had been placed under the guardianship of his uncle, Adolf Frederick of Holstein, Bishop of Lübeck. After making initial inquiries about the child's fate, Elizabeth had never really dealt with him. She suddenly felt obliged to make a sacrifice to the family spirit and to make up for lost time. As for the uncle-bishop, there could be no problem. But what would she say to the Russians? Oh well, this would hardly be the first time that a sovereign who was three-fourths a foreigner would be offered for their veneration! As soon as Elizabeth set her mind to this plan, committing the entire country to support her, secret negotiations began between Russia and Germany.

Despite the usual precautions, rumors of these talks quickly spread through the foreign ministries all across Europe. La Chétardie panicked and hunted around desperately for a way to head off this new Germanic invasion. Surmising that certain portions of the public would be hostile to her plan, Elizabeth decided to burn her bridges: without informing Bestuzhev or the Senate, she dispatched Baron Nicholas Korf to Kiel in order to bring back the "heir to the crown." She did not even bother to make inquiries beforehand to find out how the youth had turned out. As the son of her beloved sister, he would have to have inherited the most delightful personality and visual characteristics. She looked forward to this meeting with all the emotion of an expectant mother, impatient to lay eyes on the son that Heaven was about to present to her after a long gestation.

Baron Korf conducted his mission with such discretion that Peter Ulrich's arrival in St. Petersburg on February 5, 1742, almost went unnoticed by the hangers-on at the imperial Court. Seeing her nephew for the first time, Elizabeth, who had been prepared to feel a lightning bolt of maternal admiration, froze in consternation. In place of the charming adolescent Adonis that she had expected, here stood a skinny, scowling, runty fool who only spoke German, could not put two thoughts together, had a habit of laughing in an insinuating way and walked about with the look of a cornered fox. Was this the gift that she was about to spring upon an unsuspecting Russia?

Stifling her dismay, Elizabeth showed a good face to the newcomer, awarded him with the medal of St. Andrew, and appointed tutors to teach him Russian; and she asked Father Simon Todorsky to instruct him in the basics of the Orthodox religion, which would be his from now on.

Russia's Francophiles were already concerned that the admission of the crown prince to the palace would strengthen Germany's hand against France in the contest for influence. The Russophiles, clearly xenophobic, were disturbed that the tsarina still retained certain prestigious military leaders of foreign origin like the prince of Hesse-Homburg and the English generals Peter de Lascy and James Keith. Now, such high level émigrés, who had clearly demonstrated their loyalty in the past, should have been above suspicion. One had to hope that sooner or later, in Russia as elsewhere, common sense would prevail over the proponents of extremism. Unfortunately, this viewpoint was not very widespread.

La Chétardie's minister, Amelot de Chailloux, was certain that Russia was "sliding from their grasp;" to reassure him, La Chétardie reaffirmed that despite appearances "France enjoys a warm welcome here."[5] But Amelot did not have La Chétardie's reasons for succumbing to Elizabeth's charms. He did not see Russia as a power to be treated as an equal anymore; and he considered that it would be dangerous to count on the promises of a ruler as fickle as the empress. His hands tied by his recent commitments to Sweden, he preferred not to have to choose between the two and sought to stay out of their dispute, thus compromising his future neither with St. Petersburg nor with Stockholm. France prayed that the situation would resolve itself, and in the meantime played both sides of the game, making plans to bolster Sweden by arming Turkey and by supporting the Tatars against Ukraine; and all the while, Louis XV was assuring Elizabeth, via his ambassador, that he entertained feelings of fraternal understanding towards the "daughter of Peter the Great." Despite the disappointing history of her relationship with Paris and Versailles, the tsarina gave in one more time to the seduction of that strange nation whose language and spirit were so alluring. Never forgetting that she had just missed being wed to this partner with whom she now wanted to sign a formal treaty of alliance, she refused to believe that France, ever so ready with a smile and ever so slick in getting away, could be playing a double game.

Her confidence in the promises of the French did not, however, prevent her from proclaiming that no threat, from any quarter, would ever force her to yield an inch of Russian soil for, she said, her father's conquests were "more precious to her than her own life." Having convinced her compatriots to accept her, she was now anxious to persuade the nearby states that she was firmly enthroned; and she believed that a formal coronation ceremony would do more for her international reputation than any gossip among diplomats. Once the religious solemnities in the Kremlin were over, no one would dare to dispute her legitimacy nor to confront her power. To lend further weight to the ceremony, she decided to bring along her nephew so that, in his role as recognized heir, he could attend the coronation of his aunt Elizabeth I. Peter Ulrich had just turned 14; he was old enough to understand the importance of the event that was so carefully being prepared.

More than a month before the beginning of the festivities in Moscow, all the palaces and embassies in St. Petersburg emptied out (as was the custom in such instances), flowing like a tide to the tsars' old capital. An army of carriages took to the road, which was already threatening to soften in the waning winter. Some say there were 20,000 horses and 30,000 passengers at the very least, accompanied by a caravan of wagons transporting dishes, bed linens, furniture, mirrors, food and clothing — enough to furnish men and women alike for several weeks of receptions and official balls.

On March 11, Elizabeth departed from her residence at Tsarskoye Selo, having taken a few days' rest before tackling the wearying tasks that come with triumph. A special carriage was built to enable her to enjoy every conceivable convenience during the journey — which was expected to last nearly a month, taking into account the frequent stops. The vehicle was upholstered in green and was bright and airy, with broad picture windows on both sides. It was so spacious that a card table and chairs could be set up, along with a sofa and a heating stove. This traveling house was pulled by a team of twelve horses; twelve more trotted along behind, to facilitate the changes at every stage. By night, the road was lit by hundreds of resin torches placed at intervals along the route. The entrance of every insignificant village was marked by a festive gateway decorated with greenery. As the imperial carriage approached, the inhabitants, who were lined up in their holiday garb (men on one side, women on the other), bowed down to the ground, blessing the appearance of Her Majesty by making the sign of the cross and cheering Her with wishes for a long life. Whenever the cavalcade came within sight of a monastery, the bells would ring and the monks and nuns would come out of their sanctuaries in a procession to display their most prized icons before the daughter of Peter the Great.

Elizabeth never tired of the repetition of this folksy homage; to her, it already seemed like just a pleasant routine. Still, she did permit herself a few days' respite at Vsesvyatskoye before completing the trip. At dawn on April 17, 1741 she made her entrance into Moscow, with every bell in the city chiming a greeting. On April 23, heralds proclaimed at the crossroads the news of the upcoming coronation. Two days later, announced by a salvo of artillery fire, the procession was formed.

In a gesture of supreme coquetry towards France, to which she still had no lasting ties, Elizabeth had entrusted to a Frenchman by the name of Rochambeau the responsibility for ensuring the elegance and brilliance of the event. To get from the famous "red staircase" that decorated the façade of her palace to the Cathedral of the Assumption across the plaza inside the Kremlin, she advanced, hieratic, under a canopy. Twenty pages in white livery embroidered in gold carried her train. Every region of the empire was represented by its delegates, who made up a silent but colorful escort, matching its pace to that of the priests at the head of the procession. The Reverend Father Ambroise, assisted by Stephan, Bishop of Pskov, made the sign of the cross and welcomed the procession into the immense nave. Sprinkled with holy water, enveloped in the fumes of incense, Elizabeth accepted the sacramental signs of the apotheosis with a studied blend of dignity and humility. The liturgy proceeded according to an immutable rite: it was the very one that had honored Peter the Great, Catherine I and, barely eleven years ago, the pitiful Anna Ivanovna who was guilty of trying to pull the throne out from under the only woman who now had the right to sit on it.

The religious ceremonies relating to the coronation were followed by the traditional rejoicing. For eight days, illuminations, feasts and free wine were given to the crowds, while the more distinguished guests dashed from ball to banquet to masquerade. Carried away by the atmosphere of sincere cordiality with which she was surrounded, Elizabeth distributed further benefices to those who had served her so well. Alexander Buturlin was named a general and governor of Smaller Russia, while shimmering titles — count, chamberlain — rained down upon obscure relatives belonging to the maternal branch of the empress's family. The Skavronskys, Hendrikovs, and Yefimovskys were elevated from the status of wealthy peasants to newly-recognized nobles. It was as if Elizabeth, to excuse her own very great pleasure, were trying to make everyone, each in his own corner, as happy as she was on this wonderful day.

However, in Moscow such festivities and the accompanying fireworks significantly increased the risk of fire. Thus it was that one fine evening the Golovin Palace, where Her Majesty had elected to reside temporarily, caught fire. By chance, only the walls and the furniture were burned. This little accident didn't slow the revelers down one bit. A new structure was immediately raised on the half-charred ruins and while it was hastily being rebuilt and refurnished, Elizabeth moved to another house that she maintained in Moscow, at the edge of the Yauza River, and then to another of her houses in the village of Pokrovskoye, five versts away, which had belonged to an uncle of Peter the Great. Some 900 people would gather on a daily basis to celebrate with her, dancing, feasting and laughing, and the theaters did not go dark for a single night.

However, while the court was applauding an opera, *The Clemency of Titus*, by the German director Johann-Adolf Hasse, and an allegorical ballet illustrating the return of "The Golden Age" to Russia, La Chétardie was terrified to learn that a letter addressed by Amelot de Chailloux to the French ambassador in Turkey had been intercepted by the Austrian secret service; the letter contained insulting criticism against the tsarina and prophesized the collapse of the Russian Empire, "which cannot help but dissolve into complete nothingness." Horrified by this diplomatic blunder, the silver-tongued La Chétardie hoped that he could find a way to attenuate its impact on the mood of the very sensitive empress; but she felt deeply wounded by the minister's *faux pas*. Lestocq intervened, making valiant efforts to defend France by asserting that La Chétardie and Amelot were devoted to the idea of a French-Russian agreement, but Elizabeth refused to take the bait this time. She had finally lost confidence entirely in the ambassador and the country that he represented. When La Chétardie arrived, to plead his innocence in a misunderstanding that he "deplored and renounced" as much as she did, Elizabeth kept him waiting for two hours in her antechamber, among her ladies of honor; then she came out of her private apartments to tell him that she could receive him neither that day nor in the days to come, and that henceforth he would have to address himself to her foreign minister, in other words to Alexis Bestuzhev, since "Russia does not need, Sir, any intermediary" in dealing with any country whatsoever.

Despite the severe put-down, La Chétardie clung to the hope that a reconciliation could be effected. He protested, he wrote to his government, and he begged Lestocq to intercede with Her Majesty Elizabeth I once more. Didn't she have full confidence in his prescriptions, be they medical or diplomatic? Lestocq had, sometimes, provided medicines that seemed to be effective against the mild complaints from which she suffered, but his political exhortations fell flat. Elizabeth had stopped listening; she was stony in her resentment. All that La Chétardie managed to secure, with all his maneuvering, was the opportunity to have a private audience with her. He went in with the intention of redeeming himself with a few smooth words and charming smiles, but this time he hit a wall of icy scorn. Elizabeth assured him that she intended to cool Russia's relations with Versailles, while preserving her own regard and friendly feelings for a country that had shown itself incapable of appreciating her favorable disposition towards the French culture. La Chétardie withdrew, empty-handed and heavy of heart.

The ambassador's personal situation was further worsened, at that very moment, by Frederick II's abrupt about-face; he had turned his back on France, and begun to get closer to Austria. Now La Chétardie could no longer count on Mardefeld, the Prussian ambassador, to support his efforts to conclude a pact between France and Russia. His cause was lost... or was it? He suddenly had the idea of giving the throne of Courland, that had been freed up the previous year when Bühren was disgraced and exiled, to someone who was close to France — specifically, to Maurice of Saxony. And then one could go one step further — miracles are always possible on the banks of the Neva, cradle of madmen and poets! — and suggest that Saxony ask for Elizabeth's hand. If, via a French ambassador, the empress of Russia were to be married to the most brilliant military chief in the service of France, all of yesterday's minor affronts would evaporate like the morning dew. A political alliance between the two states would be replicated in a sentimental alliance that would make the union unassailable. Such a marriage would represent an unprecedented triumph, for the diplomat and for peace.

Resolving to bet everything on this last card, La Chétardie went after Maurice of Saxony; he had entered Prague as a conqueror, at the head of a French army, just a few months before.

Without revealing to him his precise plans, he urged Saxony to come quickly to Russia where, he claimed, the tsarina would be very happy to receive him. Enticed by this prestigious invitation, Maurice of Saxony could not say no. He soon arrived in Moscow, still glowing with his military successes. Elizabeth, who had long since guessed what was behind this unexpected visit, had some fun with this semi-gallant, semi-political rendezvous dreamt up by the incorrigible French ambassador. Maurice of Saxony was a handsome man and a fine talker; she was charmed by this belated suitor that La Chétardie had pulled from his sleeve. They danced together, and chatted for hours on end, in private; Elizabeth strolled about town at his side, dressed in men's clothes; watched the "commemorative" fireworks with him, and sighed languorously by the moonlit windows of the palace; but neither she nor he expressed the least sentiment that might commit them for the future. They allowed themselves to enjoy a pleasant game of flirtation, as a respite from their daily lives, both knowing that this exchange of smiles, intimate looks and compliments would lead to nothing. La Chétardie fanned the coals in vain; the fire would not take. After a few weeks of playing at love, Maurice of Saxony left Moscow to shape up his now sloppy and disorganized army, which was rumored to be on the verge of evacuating Prague.

As he headed out to achieve his destiny as a great soldier in the service of France, he wrote love letters to Elizabeth praising her beauty, her majesty, and her grace, evoking one "particularly successful" evening, a certain "white moiré gown," a certain supper where it was not the wine that was intoxicating, the nighttime ride around the Kremlin . . . She read the letters, melted, and was a little bit saddened to find herself alone again after the exaltation of this artificial courtship. When Bestuzhev advised her to enter into an alliance with England (a country that, in the opinion of the empress, had the flaw of too often being hostile to Versailles' policies), she replied that she would never be the enemy of France, "for I am too much beholden!" Whom could she have had in mind, in making a pronouncement that so exposed her intimate feelings? Louis XV, whom she had never met, to whom she had been promised in marriage only by chance and who so often had betrayed her confidence? The crafty La Chétardie who, likewise, was about to leave her? Her obscure governess, Mme. Latour, or the part-time tutor, Mr. Rambour, who in her youth at Ismailovo had taught her the subtleties of the French language? Or Maurice of Saxony, who penned such beautiful love letters but whose heart remained cold?

La Chétardie was at last recalled by his government, and he was preparing for his final audience before leaving the palace when Elizabeth called him in and spontaneously suggested that he accompany her on the pilgrimage she wished to make to the [Holy Trinity] Troitsky-St. Sergievsky Monastery, just north of Moscow.* Flattered by this return to grace, the ambassador traveled with her to this high holy place. Lodged very comfortably with the tsarina's retinue, he did not leave her side for eight days. To be frank, Elizabeth was delighted by this discreet "companionship." She took La Chétardie with her to visit the churches as well as in the drawing rooms. The courtiers were already whispering that the "Gaulois" was about to replace Maurice of Saxony in Her Majesty's favor.

But, as soon as the little imperial band returned to St. Petersburg, La Chétardie had to admit that once more he had begun to rejoice too soon. Getting a hold on herself after a brief and very feminine lapse, Elizabeth once again took a very cool, even distant, tone with La Chétardie, as in their earlier conversations. Time

---

*Ed. note: This was one of the earliest and most influential religious centers in Russia and, indeed, helped to concentrate power in Moscow during the Middle Ages.

and again, she made appointments with him and then broke them, and one day when he complained to her about Bestuzhev, whose ostracism of France was close to an obsession (according to the Fernchman), she set him in his place with a few sharp words. "We do not condemn people before proving their crimes!"[6] However, the day before La Chétardie's departure, she sent him a snuffbox studded with diamonds, with her portrait in miniature in the middle.

The day after this necessary separation from a character who charmed and irritated her by turns, Elizabeth was as sad as if she had lost a dear friend. While La Chétardie was stopped at a stagehouse along the way, an emissary from Elizabeth caught up with him. The man handed him a note in a sealed envelope, bearing only the words: "France will be in my heart forever."[7] That sounds like the wail of a lover who has been forsaken — but by whom? By an ambassador? By a king? By France itself? Her feelings must have been quite confused, by now. While her subjects may have been entitled to dream, that innocent diversion was off limits for her. Abandoned by someone whom she had always claimed was of no importance, it was time to come back to reality and to focus on the succession to the throne, rather than thinking about her life as a woman.

On November 7, 1742, she published a proclamation solemnly dubbing Duke Charles Peter Ulrich of Holstein-Gottorp Grand Duke, crown prince and Imperial Highness, under the Russian name of Peter Fyodorovich. She took this occasion to confirm her intention not to marry. In fact, she was afraid that if she married a man of lower rank, or a foreign prince, she would be letting down not only the brave men of the *Leib-Kompania* but all the Russians who were so attached to the memory of her father, Peter the Great. Better to remain unwed, she thought. To be worthy of the role that she intended to play, she would have to forego any union officially sanctioned by the Church and remain faithful to her image as the maiden-tsar, "the imperial Virgin," already celebrated by Russian legend.

On the other hand, she was beginning to see that the youth whom she had selected to be her heir, whom she had had baptized into the Orthodox faith under the name of Peter Fyodorovich and who had so very little Russian blood in his veins, was never going to forget his true fatherland. In fact, despite the efforts of his mentor, Simon Todorsky, Grand Duke Peter always returned instinctively to his origins. Besides, it was hard not to continue worshiping his native Germany when everything about the society, the streets and the shops of St. Petersburg reflected its influence so strongly. It was clear that the majority of influential people in the palace and in the ministries spoke German more fluently than Russian, and along the very luxurious Nevsky Prospect, many of the stores were German; elsewhere, signs of the Hanseatic League were in evidence, and there were plenty of Lutheran churches. When Peter Fyodorovich showed up at a barracks guardroom, during a walk about town, the officer he addressed would often answer him in German. And with every reminder of his homeland, Peter regretted being exiled in this city that, despite its splendors, meant less to him than the most trivial village of Schleswig-Holstein.

Forced to acclimatize himself, he took an aversion to the Russian vocabulary, Russian grammar, and Russian ways. He resented Russia for not being German, and he took to saying, "I was not born for the Russians, and I do not like them!" Living at the center of this great land of foreigners, he chose his friends from among the declared Germanophiles, and put together a little homeland to console himself. He surrounded himself with a close circle of sympathizers, and pretended to live with them in Russia as if their mission were to colonize that backward and uncultivated country.

Elizabeth looked on helplessly as this young man, whom she had sought to forcibly integrate into a nation where he felt completely out of place, developed an obsession. Apparently, a sovereign's so-called absolute power has its limits. Believing she had acted for the good of all, she wondered whether she had not made the gravest error in her life in entrusting the future of Peter the Great's empire to a prince who clearly hated both Russia and the Russians.

Footnotes

1. Cited by Daria Olivier, *op. cit.*
2. *Ibid.*
3. Letter dated 27 February 1742 ; cf. Brian-Chaninov, *op. cit.*
4. Letters from Mardefeld, dated 12 and 19 December 1741, quoted by Simievski: "Élisabeth Petrovna", in *Parole russe*, 1859, cited by K. Waliszewski in *La Dernière des Romanov, Élisabeth Ire*.
5. Letter dated 16 December 1741 ; cf. Daria Olivier, *op. cit.*
6. Cf. Daria Olivier, *op. cit.*
7. *Ibid.*

VIII

An Autocrat at Work and Play

Elizabeth's main challenge was to enjoy herself fully without neglecting the interests of Russia too much. That was a difficult balance to achieve in a world where temptations, romantic and otherwise, were rife. Given Louis XV's obstinate refusal to extend a hand to her, should she not rather follow her nephew's example and seek the friendship of Prussia, which was more favorably disposed to her? Although her adoptive son was just 15 years old, she felt it was time to give some thought to finding him a bride — a German bride, preferably — or at least one who had been born and raised on Frederick II's territory. At the same time, she still preserved the hope that good relations could be restored with Versailles; she charged her ambassador, Prince Kantemir, with discreetly notifying the king that she regretted the marquis of La Chétardie's departure and that she would be happy to receive him at her court again. He had been replaced in St. Petersburg by an ambassador plenipotentiary, Mr. d'Usson d'Allion, a strait-laced character whom the empress found neither attractive nor impressive.

With the French continually letting her down, she comforted herself by imitating (in her own way) the fads and fashions of that country that she so admired. This fancy resulted in an unrestrained passion for clothing, jewels, bibelots and conversational tics that seemed to have a Parisian cachet. She never missed a chance to round out her wardrobe; indeed, since dancing made her perspire profusely, she would change her garb three times during a ball. As soon as a French ship arrived in the port of St. Petersburg, she would have the cargo inspected; and the latest innovations of Parisian dressmakers were brought to her first, so that none of her subjects might know the latest fashions before her. Her favorite gowns were of colorful silk, preferably overlaid with gold or silver embroidery; but she would also dress as a man to surprise her entourage by the pleasing contour of her calves and her trim ankles. Twice a week, a masquerade ball was held at the court. Her Majesty would participate, in the costume of a Cossack *hetman*, a Louis XIII musketeer, or a Dutch sailor. Judging that she was more attractive in male clothing than any of her usual female guests, she instituted masked balls where the women were required to dress in Parisian-style jackets and knee-breeches and the men in skirts with panniers.

She was overweaningly jealous of other women's beauty and could not brook the slightest competition. Once, she arrived at a ball wearing a rose in her hair, only to notice with indignation that Madame Natalya Lopukhin, famous for her social successes, was also wearing one. No mere coincidence, thought Elizabeth; she considered it an obvious attack upon the imperial honor. Stopping the orchestra in the middle of a minuet, she made Mrs. Lopukhin kneel, called for a pair of scissors, furiously clipped the offending flower and the tresses that had been cleverly curled around the stem, slapped the unfortunate woman on both cheeks in front of a group of stunned courtiers, and signaled to the orchestra to go on with the dance. At the end of the piece, somebody whispered in her ear that Mrs. Lopukhin had fainted with shame. Shrugging, the tsarina muttered, "She only got what she deserved, the imbecile!" And immediately after taking this little revenge, she returned to her usual serene mood, as if it had been some other person who had been so upset just a moment before. Similarly, during a trip through the countryside Aksakov, one of her last buffoons, thought it would be funny to show her a porcupine in his hat — he had just captured it, alive; Elizabeth shrieked with horror, fled to her tent, and gave orders for the insolent entertainer to be tortured to death for the crime of "having frightened Her Majesty."[1]

These disproportionate reprisals were counterbalanced by sudden exercises of religious devotion; she could be easily enraged or spontaneously repentant. She would take it upon herself to make pilgrimages, on foot, to various holy places, testing the limits of her strength. She would stand for hours on end during church services, and she observed fasts scrupulously, to the point of sometimes fainting after leaving the table without having eaten anything. The following day she would suffer from indigestion while trying to make up for lost time. Her conduct was excessive and unpredictable. She enjoyed surprising others and being surprised, herself (only, not with porcupines). She was chaotic, odd, and only half-civilized. She scorned fixed schedules, was as quick to punish as to forget, fraternized with those of humble station and sneered at the great. She had a habit of dropping in at the kitchen to enjoy the smells of the simmering dishes. She would laugh or shout unexpectedly, and gave those who knew her well the impression of being an old-fashioned housewife whose taste for French frills had not stifled her healthy Slavic rusticity.

In Peter the Great's day, the courtiers had had to suffer

through "assemblies" convoked by the tsar in order to introduce his subjects to Western customs. They were more like tedious meetings of poorly-groomed aristocrats, condemned by the Reformer to obey, to dissimulate and to show obeisance. Under Anna Ivanovna, these assemblies had deteriorated into nests of intrigue and worry. Unspoken fear was rampant, under the mask of courtesy. The shadow of the devilish Bühren was on the prowl. And now a princess who loved dressing up, dancing, and playing games was insisting that they come to her palace purely for enjoyment's sake. Certainly, the Empress was known to have fits of anger sometimes, or to come up with strange innovations, but all her guests had to admit that, for the first time, the palace was suffused with a blend of Russian good-naturedness and Parisian elegance. Instead of being a chore, these visits to the temple of monarchy finally seemed to offer an occasion to enjoy oneself socially.

Not satisfied with organizing "new style" events at her own many residences, Elizabeth obliged the greatest families of the empire to host masked balls, in turn, under their own roofs. The French ballet master de Landet taught everyone at court the graceful moves of the minuet. He soon made the claim that, under his direction, gallantry and civility were more in evidence along the Neva than anywhere else in the world. The parties would start at one mansion or another at 6:00 in the evening; dancing and card-playing would go on until ten o'clock. Then the Empress, surrounded by certain favored individuals, would sit down at table for supper; the other guests would eat standing up, elbow to elbow, struggling to avoid dropping anything on their fancy clothes. Once Her Majesty had downed her last mouthful, the dancing would begin again; and it would go on until 2:00 in the morning. To please in the leading lady, the menu would be both abundant and refined. Her Majesty liked French cuisine and her chefs (first Fornay, and then Füchs, an Alsatian) were paid 800 rubles per annum to make it a success at these great suppers. Elizabeth's admiration for Peter the Great stopped short of imitating his enthusiasm for enormous feasts and drink-to-death binges; however, she did inherit his appreciation for the robust national gastronomy. Her favorite dishes, aside from gala feasts, were *blini*, *kulebiaka* and buckwheat kasha. At the solemn banquets of the *Leib-Kompania*, which she would attend dressed as a captain of the regiment, she would give the signal to drink by emptying large glasses of vodka in one draught.

This penchant for rich food and strong drink conferred upon Her Majesty a premature plumpness and annoying red blotches on the cheeks. After eating and drinking her fill, she would allow herself to nap for an hour or two. To facilitate this rest, a kind of sleepy meditation, she employed the services of a few women who would take turns sitting by her side, speaking softly and scratching the bottoms of her feet. Elizabeth Ivanovna Shuvalov, the sister of Her Majesty's new lover Ivan Shuvalov, was a specialist in this soporific tickling. She would hear all the tsarina's confidences during these foot-rubbing sessions, so that she began to be known at the court as "the real Minister of Foreign Affairs." When the tsarina had finished resting, the foot-scratchers would give way to the favorite of the moment. Sometimes that was Ivan Shuvalov, sometimes the chamberlain Basil Chulkov, sometimes Her Majesty's eternal suitor Simon Naryshkin, sometimes Shubin (a private in her guard), and sometimes the indestructible and ever so accommodating Alexis Razumovsky, the most assiduous and honored of all.

The people around Elizabeth called him "the night emperor." She often deceived him, but in the end she could never stand to give him up. Only in his arms could she feel that she was both dominant and dominated at the same time. He had a deep voice, and used to be the cantor in the imperial chapel; he spoke with a heavy Ukrainian accent, only said simple things, and — a rarity in the tsarina's entourage — never asked for favors. At most he consented to have his mother, Natalya Demianovna, share the fortune that he was enjoying. He was concerned that contact with the court would harm a woman of her condition, accustomed to discretion and poverty. Natalya Demianovna's first visit to the palace was an event. Seeing this *muzhik*'s widow stepping into her apartments, wedged into a formal gown, Elizabeth forgot all modesty and exclaimed with gratitude, "Blessed be the fruit of your entrails!" But her lover's mother was not an ambitious woman. Hardly having been named lady-in-waiting and installed in the palace, "Razumikhina"[2], as she was contemptuously called behind her back, requested permission to leave the court. Returning to obscurity, sheltered from scandalmongers, she once again donned her peasant clothing.

Alexis Razumovsky understood very well how frightened this "woman of the people" must have been by the excesses of those at the top. He insisted that Her Majesty spare his mother the signs of honor that others around her were so keen to receive. As for himself, in spite of his rising stature and fortune, he refused to consider himself worthy of the good fortune that had come to him. The more his influence over Elizabeth increased, the less he wished to be involved in politics.

His lack of interest in intrigues and rewards only gave his imperial mistress greater confidence in him. She made many public appearances with him, and she was proud of this companion whose only claim to respect from the nation were the titles that she had given him. When she presented him she was presenting *her own* handiwork, her personal Russia that she offered to her contemporaries for their assessment. He owed his elevation to her, and she was gratified to see her favorite receiving further honors. Scornful as he was of official distinctions, she was delighted, as much for herself as for him, when he was named count of the Holy Roman Empire by Charles VII. When she made him a field marshal, he smiled ironically and thanked her in terms that give a clear picture of the man he was: "Liz, you can do whatever you like, but you will never make anyone take me seriously, even as a simple lieutenant."[3]

Soon, all the court considered Razumovsky not only the "night emperor" but a Prince Consort, as legitimate as if his union with Elizabeth had been consecrated by a priest. Moreover, rumors had been circulating for months that they had married, in great secrecy, in the church of the little village of Perovo, outside of Moscow. The couple supposedly had been blessed by Father Dubiansky, the empress's chaplain and guardian of her deepest secrets. No courtier attended these clandestine nuptials. Nothing changed, outwardly, in the tsarina's relations with her favorite. If Elizabeth had wanted this secret sacrament, it was simply to keep God on her side. Debauched and unruly as her lifestyle was, she needed to believe that the Almighty was with her in her everyday life and in her exercise of power. This illusion of a supernatural partnership helped her maintain some semblance of equilibrium in the midst of the many contradictions that shook her from all sides.

From that day forward, Razumovsky visited her at night with impunity. This new situation should have encouraged them to exchange political opinions with as much ease and confidence as their caresses, but Razumovsky was still hesitant to abandon his neutrality. However, while he never imposed his will on Elizabeth when it came to making fundamental decisions, she was well aware of his preferences. Guided by his instinct as a man of the earth, he was generally supportive of Chancellor Bestuzhev's nationalist ideas. In such times, when some states are at war and others are preparing for it, and when forging alliances is the principal occupation of all the foreign ministries, it was difficult to see clearly where Russia's best interests lay. What is clear, in any case, is that the hostilities between Russia and Sweden (recklessly started in 1741 under the regency of Anna Leopoldovna) came to an end. The Russians, led by Generals Lascy and Keith, won several victories over the Swedes and a peace agreement was signed on August 8, 1743. Via the treaty of Abo, Russia gave back some recently conquered territories but held onto most of Finland. With the Swedish conflict settled, Elizabeth hoped that France would prove less hostile to the idea of an accord. But, in the meantime, St. Petersburg had signed a pact of friendship with Berlin, which Versailles took very badly. Once again, every attempt would have to be made to assuage, reassure, and persuade them of Russia's good faith.

It was on the background of this unsettled international context that an affair erupted that neither Bestuzhev nor Elizabeth had been prepared for in the least. In mid-summer, St. Petersburg was rocked by rumors of a plot being fomented among the highest nobility, intended to overthrow Elizabeth I, at the instigation of the Austrian ambassador Botta d'Adorno. This disloyal and disruptive coterie was said to be considering offering the throne to the Brunswick family, gathered around little Ivan VI. As soon as Elizabeth got wind of this, she ordered the impudent Botta d'Adorno arrested. But, having a good nose for danger, he had already left Russia. He was said to be on his way to Berlin, on the way to Austria.

This diplomatic felon may have escaped, but his Russian accomplices were still around. The most compromised were those who were close (or distant) relations of the Lopukhin clan. Elizabeth didn't forget that she had had to slap Natalya Lopukhin for having the temerity to wear a rose in her hair. Moreover, her rival had been the mistress of Loewenwolde, recently exiled to Siberia. But there were other members of the conspiracy who were even more despicable. At the top of the list Elizabeth put Mrs. Mikhail Bestuzhev, née Golovkin, sister of a former vice-chancellor and sister-in-law of the current chancellor Alexis Bestuzhev, and widow, by her first marriage, of one of Peter the Great's closest associates, Yaguzhinsky.

While waiting for the Russian culprits to be arrested and tried, she hoped that Austria would punish its ambassador severely. But, while King Frederick II expelled Botta as soon as he arrived in Berlin, the empress Maria Theresa, having welcomed the diplomat in Vienna, merely scolded him. Disappointed by the feeble reactions of two foreign sovereigns whom she had believed were more solid in their monarchical convictions, Elizabeth took revenge by locking up the princely couple of Brunswick and their son, young Ivan VI, in the maritime fortress of Dunamunde, on the Duna, where she could keep a closer eye on them than in Riga. She also considered dismissing Alexis Bestuzhev, whose family was so compromised. Then, no doubt under Razumovsky's influence in favor of moderation, she allowed the chancellor to retain his post.

However, she needed victims on whom to vent her fury, and she chose to make Mrs. Lopukhin, her Ivan son and some of their close relatives take the brunt of it. For Natalya Lopukhin, a slap in the face was no longer punishment enough; this time, she was in for horrible torture — and her accomplices as well. Under the knout, the clippers and the branding iron, Lopukhin, her son Ivan, and Mrs. Bestuzhev, writhing in pain, repeated the calumnies that they had heard from the mouth of Botta. In spite of the lack of material evidence, a hastily convened emergency court (made up of several members of the Senate and three representatives of the clergy) sentenced all the "culprits" to the wheel, quartering, and decapitation. This exemplary sentence offered Elizabeth the opportunity to decide, during a ball, that she would spare life of the miserable wretches who had dared to conspire against her, and would limit their punishment to public "lesson." When this extraordinary measure of leniency was announced, everyone present cheered Her Majesty's angelic kindness.

On August 31, 1743, a scaffold was erected in front of the palace of Colleges. Standing before an enormous crowd of curious onlookers, Mrs. Mikhail Bestuzhev was brutally stripped by the torturer. As she had managed to find the time to slip him a jewel-studded cross just before he began, he barely stroked her back with the whip and slid his knife over her tongue without scratching the flesh. She suffered these apparent blows and wounds with heroic dignity. Less sure of her nerves, Mrs. Lopukhin struggled desperately when the torturer's assistant ripped off her clothes. The multitude was stunned to silence by the suddenly revealed nudity of this woman who was even more appealing in her distress. Then some of witnesses, impatient to see the rest, began to howl. Panicking at this outburst of raw hatred, the poor woman struggled, insulted the torturer and bit his hand. Furious, he grabbed her by the throat, forced open her jaws, held up the sacrificial weapon and presented the laughing crowd with a bloody scrap of meat. "Who'll take the tongue of the beautiful Mrs. Lopukhin?," he cried. "It is a lovely piece, and I am selling it cheap! One ruble for the tongue of the beautiful Mrs. Lopukhin!"[4] This was a common type of joke from executioners in those days, but this time the public paid more attention than usual, for Natalya Lopukhin had just fainted from pain and horror. The torturer revived her with a large knout. When she came to her senses, she was thrown into a carriage and shipped off to Siberia! Her husband would soon join her in Seleguinsky, after being severely whipped, himself. He died there a few years later in a state of to-tal abandonment. As for the Bestuzhevs, Madame lingered on for many miserable years in Yakutsk, suffering a life of hunger, cold and the indifference of her neighbors (who were reluctant to com-promise themselves by looking after someone who had been re-jected) while, in St. Petersburg, her husband Mikhail Bestuzhev (brother of Chancellor Alexis Bestuzhev) went on with his diplo-matic career, and their daughter was a reigning beauty at Her Majesty's court.

In settling the Botta matter, Elizabeth thought she had gained control over the volatile situation within her empire. Alexis Bestuzhev, having preserved his ministerial prerogatives in spite of the disgrace that had befallen most of his kin, had reason to think that his prestige had even been enhanced. However, in Versailles, Louis XV persisted in his intention to send La Chétar-die on a reconnaissance mission to the tsarina, who (according to his advisors) would not mind engaging in a playful new fencing bout with a Frenchman whose gallantries she had once found amusing. But she was so flighty that, according to the same "experts on the Slavic soul," she was liable to be upset over a trifle and to over-react to any misstep. To spare the sensitivities of this sovereign so susceptible to changing humors, the king gave La Chétardie two letters of introduction to Her Majesty. In one, Ver-sailles's emissary was presented as an ordinary person interested in everything that related to Russia, and in the other, as a plenipo-tentiary delegated to represent the king to "our very dear sister and absolutely perfect friend Elizabeth, empress and autocrat of all the Russias."[5] La Chétardie could decide on the spot which formula was best suited to the circumstances. With this double recommendation in his pocket, how could he help but succeed?

Traveling as quickly as possible, he arrived in St. Petersburg on the very same day when the empress was celebrating the tenth

anniversary of her coup d'état. Amused by La Chétardie's eagerness to congratulate her, Elizabeth granted him a part-friendly,
part-protocol interview in the evening. She found him tired, fat-
ter, but so well-spoken that he thought he had charmed her completely, making her forget her past complaints against France.
But, just as he was preparing to deploy every seductive wile in his
possession, in came the titular Ambassador of France, Monsieur
d'Allion. Mortified by what he considered unfair competition,
d'Allion was anxious to stick an umbrella in his spokes. After a
series of harsh statements, Louis XV's two representatives exchanged insults, slapped each other, and drew their swords. Although he was wounded in the hand, La Chétardie kept his dignity. Finally, realizing how silly it was for two Frenchmen in foreign territory to quarrel, the adversaries reluctantly reconciled.

This took place just before Christmas. As it happens, it was
precisely then, at the end of 1743, that the news Elizabeth had so
much hoped for arrived from Berlin. The King of Prussia, solicited
by various emissaries to find a bride for the heir to the Russian
throne, finally presented a pearl: a princess of adequate birth,
pleasant appearance and good education, who would be a credit
to her husband without trying to eclipse him.

That was exactly the kind of daughter-in-law the empress
had dreamed of finding. The candidate, just 15 years old, was born
in Stettin; her name was Sophia of Anhalt-Zerbst (*Figchen*, to her
family). Her father, Christian Augustus of Anhalt-Zerbst, was not
even a reigning prince; he merely ruled over his small hereditary
prerogative under the condescending protection of Frederick II.
Sophia's mother, Johanna of Holstein-Gottorp, was a German
cousin of the late Charles Frederick, father of the Grand Duke Peter, whom Elizabeth had made her heir. Johanna was 27 years
younger than her husband and had great ambitions for her daugh-

ter. Elizabeth considered this all very good for the family, very German, and very promising. Just going over the genealogy of the fiancée, branch by branch, Elizabeth felt herself back on familiar ground.

While she was predisposed in favor of the young lady, she was very disappointed in her nephew, whom she had come to know all too well. Why wasn't he more interested to learn the results of the matrimonial maneuvers that had been conducted in his behalf? The principal interested party, too, was kept out of the negotiations of which she was the object. Everything was agreed through confidential correspondence between Zerbst (where Sophia's parents resided), Berlin (where Frederick II was headquartered), and St. Petersburg (where the empress was anxiously awaiting the news from Prussia).

All the information she was able to obtain concurred: according to the few people who had met the girl, she was gracious, cultivated and reasonable, spoke French as well as German, and, despite her tender years, conducted herself well under any circumstance. Too good to be true? Seeing Figchen's portrait, sent by Frederick II, Elizabeth was even more convinced. The little princess was truly delicious, with a sweet face and an innocent look.

Fearing any last-minute disappointment, the tsarina kept secret from her entourage the imminence of the great event that she was preparing for the happiness of Russia. But, while Alexis Bestuzhev may have been in the dark, diplomats close to Prussia were well aware of what was going on, and they found it hard to keep the news to themselves. Mardefeld kept La Chétardie and Lestocq informed as the talks progressed day by day. Here and there, rumors began to circulate. The Francophile clan was guardedly optimistic to hear that this princess, educated by a French teacher, was coming to join the court. She might be Prussian by blood, but she could not help but serve the cause of France if she had been well-instructed by her governess — even if the marriage plans fell through.

Elizabeth received news of Sophia's progress en route to the capital, with her mother. They presented themselves in Berlin, where they received Frederick II's blessing and bankrupted themselves buying a suitable trousseau. Sophia's father stayed behind in Zerbst. Was it to save money or to save face that he refused to accompany his daughter on this quest for a prestigious fiancé? Elizabeth didn't care: the fewer Prussian relations surrounding the girl, the better it would be. She sent the ladies an allowance to help defray their travel expenses, and suggested that they remain *incognito* at least until they arrived in Russia. When they crossed the border, they were to say that they were on their way to St. Petersburg to pay Her Majesty a courtesy call. The tsarina had a comfortable carriage, drawn by six horses, waiting for them when they got to Riga. They gratefully wrapped themselves in the sable shawls that Elizabeth had thoughtfully provided against the chill, and continued their journey north.

However, upon their arrival in St. Petersburg, , they were disconcerted to learn that the Empress and all the court had removed to Moscow in order to celebrate Grand Duke Peter's 17th birthday on February 10, 1744. In Elizabeth's absence, La Chétardie and the Prussian ambassador, Mardefeld, had been left to welcome the ladies and introduce them to the capital city.

Sophia was enchanted by the beauty of this enormous city built at the water's edge, admired the regiments' changing of the guard and clapped her hands with pleasure at the sight of fourteen elephants, a gift to Peter the Great from the shah of Persia. Her shrewd mother, however, was miffed that they had not yet been presented to the Empress. She was also worried by Chancellor Alexis Bestuzhev's frosty attitude toward the intended match. She knew he was "more Russian than Russia itself," and violently opposed to any concession to the interests of Prussia. Furthermore, she had heard rumors that he intended to induce the Holy Synod to oppose the marriage on the basis that the two fiancés were too closely related. Elizabeth was unfazed by Johanna's worries: she knew that at the first hint from her, Bestuzhev would drop his objections and fall into line, for fear of setting off another wave of punishment against his clan, and she knew that the high prelates, mumbling in their beards, would bite their tongues and go ahead to give the couple their blessing.

Johanna cut short her daughter's fun and entertainment and, on Mardefeld's advice, set off at the end of January to meet the court in Moscow. La Chétardie escorted them. Elizabeth had set a date to receive them at the Annenhof Palace, in the eastern sector of the second capital, on February 9 at 8:00pm. After keeping them waiting, she gave orders to open the doors to the audience hall and appeared at the threshold, while the two visitors sank into their deepest curtseys. She took in the future fiancée in a glance — a slender, pale young girl, in a pink and silver gown with a plain skirt — no pannier. The toilette was inadequate but the girl herself was darling. Standing next to this scrumptious young lady, Peter — who had come to take delivery of this princess that had been shipped to him — looked even uglier and more disagreeable than usual.

His provocations recently had reached a new height, as he had taken up with Brummer, the minister from Holstein, and a clique of schemers all of German extraction. Furthermore, instead of being pleased that Her Majesty had named him a colonel in the Preobrazhensky Regiment, he now had the gall to invite a regiment from Holstein to come and demonstrate what was meant by discipline and efficiency — two qualities that were, in his view, sorely lacking in the Russian military.

Elizabeth had long mourned her inability to produce an heir for Russia herself, but given all these annoyances from her Germanophile nephew she must have been glad, in the end, that he was in fact not her own son. This disastrous successor resembled her neither in mind nor spirit. She began to pity the poor girl she was about to throw at the feet of such an unworthy man. She would have to do whatever she could to help the new bride win over, and control, the stupid and fanatical young fellow who was destined to become emperor one day. If only Sophia could still rely on her mother to guide her and comfort her in her disappointment; but with all her airs, Johanna appeared to be as irksome as Sophia was pleasing, with her aura of sincerity, health and good cheer.

Some relationships can be sized up in a flash. Elizabeth sensed that the bond between Johanna and Sophia was more form than feeling, based on circumstance and need rather than on affection and sympathy. Maybe Elizabeth could take the girl in hand; maybe it would be a pleasure to do so. While she had not been able to do much to mold the Grand Duke, perhaps she could help Sophia to develop into a happy, clear-headed and independent woman — without impinging on the husband's traditional authority.

As a start, she had Razumovsky bring her the insignia of the Order of St. Catherine, and had two ladies-in-waiting pin them to the bodice of Sophia's dress. Razumovsky was aware of her feelings in regard to this unequal but so necessary match, which had no hope of providing its protagonists with the satisfaction Elizabeth had found in her *de facto* marriage.

In the days that followed, Elizabeth watched closely and had her ladies-in-waiting report as well on the conduct of the young couple. While Sophia seemed to be waiting for her suitor to undertake some sort of gallant initiative, the foolish grand duke talked about nothing but the fine qualities of the Prussian Army, on parade as well as in combat, while systematically denigrating everything about Russia, from its customs to its history to its religion. Was he simply trying to assert his independence? As though in compensation, Sophia began to display the contrary view on every point, and seemed to find the history and the traditions of her new homeland more and more appealing.

Both Vasily Adadurov and Simon Todorsky, the tutors appointed by Her Majesty to instruct Sophia in the Russian language and religion, praised her diligence. Enjoying the intellectual effort, she would study the most difficult problems of vocabulary, grammar and theology until late at night. Then she caught cold, and took to bed with a fever. Terrified that they might fail in their objective, after coming so close, Johanna accused her of shirking her duties as a princess preparing herself for marriage; she told her to get up and get back to work.

The Francophile clique took this development as a positive sign. If the perspiring, shivering Sophia should fail to recover, a replacement bride would have to be found — and another candidate might be more inclined to favor an Anglo-Austrian alliance. Elizabeth hotly declared that she would refuse any Saxon candidate, come what may.

The men of medicine recommended bleeding the patient; Johanna was against it. Elizabeth, under pressure from her personal physician, Lestocq, cast the deciding vote and Sophia was bled 17 times in seven weeks. That was how they saved horses, and that is how they saved her. Back on her feet but still very weak, she went straight back into the fray.

She was to celebrate her 15th birthday on April 21, 1744, but she was so pale and thin that she was afraid she would make a poor impression on the public, and maybe even on her fiancé. Moved by an uncharacteristic solicitude, Elizabeth sent her some rouge and suggested she touch up her face in order to appear to better advantage. Impressed by Figchen's courage, she found the charming girl (who was unrelated to her, but was so eager to become Russian) far more worthy than her pitiful nephew and adoptive son (who was adamant in remaining German).

Meanwhile, Johanna was busily engaging in high politics and covert diplomacy. She received visits from all the traditional enemies of Chancellor Alexis Bestuzhev, the inveterate Russophile. La Chétardie, Lestocq and Brummer held clandestine meetings in her apartments. Perhaps Sophia, under her mother's direction, could influence Peter and maybe even the tsarina, who was visibly impressed with her, to get rid of Bestuzhev.

But Russia's top diplomat was hardly sitting idly by while these conspiracies were being spun. His personal spies had succeeded in intercepting and deciphering encrypted correspondence from La Chétardie to various foreign ministries all over Europe. With these incriminating documents in hand, he presented himself to Elizabeth to prove his case. He had a portfolio full of damning letters, which Elizabeth read with horror: "Recognition and attention from such a dissipated princess [the tsarina] mean nothing." "Her vanity, lack of seriousness, bad conduct, weakness and obstinacy make any serious negotiation an impossibility." Elsewhere, La Chétardie criticized her excessive interest in clothing and frivolous pursuits, and stated that she was totally ignorant of the major issues of the day, which she found "annoying rather than interesting." In support of these calumnies, La Chétardie cited the opinion of Johanna, whom he portrayed, furthermore, as a spy in league with Frederick II.

Elizabeth was shocked by these revelations; she no longer knew who were her friends — if, indeed, she had any. She had turned her back on Maria Theresa because of Ambassador Botta, who had called her a diplomatic crook; would she now have to part with Louis XV because of that scoundrel, La Chétardie? She ought to throw him out of the country forthwith. But wouldn't that offend France, which had to be dealt with as a man more than as a nation?

Before making such an unequivocal gesture, Elizabeth had Johanna called in and, screaming with rage and indignation, showed her the letters. Sophia's mother was directly incriminated. The young princess from Anhalt-Zerbst, stunned to see her dreams of grandeur flushed away so suddenly, expected to be chased out of Russia forthwith. However, she was granted an unexpected reprieve. Out of respect for her nephew's innocent fiancée, Elizabeth consented to allow Johanna to stay on, at least until the wedding. This charity did not cost the tsarina anything, and she felt that it would turn to her own benefit in due course. She was sorry for the young lady, who seemed to have a most unnatural mother; and she hoped, by this demonstration of generosity of soul, to earn the girl's gratitude and, perhaps, even her affection.

The deleterious climate of St. Petersburg suddenly felt intolerable to Her Majesty and, yielding to one of the mystical whims that would strike her from time tot time, she decided to make another pilgrimage to the Troitsky-St. Sergievsky Monastery. She would take her nephew, Sophia, Johanna and Lestocq. Before leaving town, she instructed Alexis Bestuzhev to deal with the ignoble La Chétardie however he saw fit, saying that she approved, in advance, of whatever action he chose to take. Having thus washed her hands of the entire sordid affair, she departed on the road to God with an unburdened heart. As the pilgrimage got under way, Elizabeth noted that, while Johanna, Sophia and Lestocq were quite upset over the awkward business of La Chétardie's letters, Peter was completely unfazed. He seemed to be quite oblivious to the fact that this scandal involved his fiancée, soon to be his wife, and that everything that involved her must affect him as well.

At the monastery, the traveling party discussed the young couple's future, in religious and not very religious terms; meanwhile, in St. Petersburg, a party of officers and armed guards presented themselves at La Chétardie's residence and informed him that, in view of his defamations against Her Majesty, he had 24 hours in which to take his leave. Kicked out like a dishonest servant, the Marquis protested, argued, raged, and claimed that he would lodge a complaint with his government; finally, he accepted his fate and quickly packed up.

When he reached the first coach house along the way, an emissary from the Empress caught up with him and demanded that he give back the Order of St. Andrew, and the snuffbox with her portrait enameled in miniature on the lid which he had received some years before — while he was in good standing with the court. He refused to part with these relics. At the next stage, Bestuzhev conveyed to him, by another courier, a comminatory sentence from Elizabeth: "The Marquis de La Chétardie is not worthy of receiving personal commissions from Her Majesty." At this sudden fall from grace, La Chétardie thought he was losing his mind. He asked Versailles to intervene in a matter that, in his view, insulted France as much as it insulted him. This time, it was Louis XV who set him in his place. As punishment for his maladroit initiatives, he should withdraw to his estate in Limousin, and stay there until further notice.

As for Elizabeth and her fellow pilgrims, after paying a pious visit to the monastery, they made their way back to Moscow where the ladies from Anhalt-Zerbst strove to appear natural in spite of their shame and disappointment. Johanna was in a rage, knowing that she was now quite unwelcome in Russia and guessing that she would be invited to take her ship out as soon as her daughter was wed. Sophia, for her part, tried to get over this series of setbacks by preparing for her conversion to orthodoxy with all the zeal of a neophyte. While she was scrupulously attending to everything said by the priest charged with initiating her into the faith of her new compatriots, Peter was off on a hunting excursion, merrily scouring the surrounding forests and plains, with his usual comrades. They were all from Holstein, they spoke only German among themselves, and they encouraged the Grand Duke to resist Russian traditions and stand fast to his Germanic origins.

On June 28, 1744, Sophia was finally received into the bosom of the Orthodox Church. She gave her baptism vows in Russian, without stumbling, and changed her first name to become Catherine Alexeyevna. She was not shocked at being required to give up her own religion — she had long understood that that was part of the price to be paid if one wished to marry a Russian of quality.

The following day, June 29, she presented herself at the imperial chapel for the engagement ceremony. The empress slowly stepped forward, under a silver canopy held aloft by eight generals. Behind her the Grand Duke Peter advanced, smiling idiotically all around, with the new Grand Duchess Catherine by his side, pale and deeply moved, her eyes lowered. The service, celebrated by Father Ambroise, was four hours long. Despite her recent illness, Catherine never faltered. Elizabeth was pleased with her future daughter-in-law. During the ball that brought the festivities to a close, Elizabeth noticed once more the contrast between the girl's elegance and simplicity and the brazenness of the mother, who talked nonstop and was always putting herself forward.

Shortly thereafter, the entire court removed to Kiev, in great array. The young couple and Johanna came behind. Once again there were receptions, balls, parades and processions and, at the end of the day, for the tsarina (accustomed as she was to the social whirl), the strange feeling of having wasted considerable time. During this three-month voyage, Elizabeth had pretended to be unaware that the world outside was on the move. England, it was said, was preparing to attack the Netherlands, while France was spoiling for a fight with Germany, and the Austrians were on the verge of confronting the French army. Versailles and Vienna were cunningly competing to secure Russia's assistance, and Alexis Bestuzhev was straddling the fence the best he could, while awaiting precise instructions from Her Majesty. The empress, alarmed no doubt by her chancellor's reports, decided to head back to Moscow. The court immediately picked up and moved, in a long, slow caravan, back to the north. Arriving at the old city of coronations, Elizabeth certainly expected to enjoy a few days of rest; she claimed to have been tired by all the celebrations in Kiev. But as soon as she took in the stimulating Moscow air, her appetite was piqued for further entertainment and surprises. At her initiative, the balls, suppers, operas and masquerades started up once again, and at such a pace that even the youngest socialites started to bow out.

As the wedding date approached, Elizabeth decided to move back to St. Petersburg to oversee the preparations. The engaged couple and Johanna followed her, a few days behind. But, stepping down from the carriage at the stage house in Khotilovo, the Grand Duke Peter began to shiver. Pink blotches had broken out on his face. There could be no doubt: it was small pox — and few people survived that dread disease. An urgent message was sent to the empress. Elizabeth was terrified, hearing of this threat to her adoptive son's life. Who could forget that, less than fifteen years earlier, the young tsar Peter II had succumbed to that very peril on the eve of his wedding? And by a strange coincidence, the bride-to-be, back in 1730, a Dolgoruky, was also called Catherine. Was that name an evil omen for the Romanov dynasty?

Elizabeth refused to believe it, just as she refused to believe that the illness would be fatal. She gave orders to prepare the horses and took off for Khotilovo, to be near her heir and to ensure that he was receiving proper care. Meanwhile Catherine, thrown into a panic, had left Khotilovo for the capital. Along the way, she came upon Elizabeth's sleigh. United by their anguish, the empress (who feared the worst for her succession), and the bride-to-be (who feared the worst for her own future) fell into each other's arms. By now, Elizabeth had no more doubt that the Good Lord had guided her to place her confidence in this diminutive 15-year-old princess. Catherine was indeed the right wife for that simpleton, Peter, and the right daughter-in-law to enable her to enjoy life and end her days in peace. They set out again for Khotilovo, together. Arriving in the village, they went to see the Grand Duke, who was racked with fever, perspiring and shivering on a miserable cot. Was this pitiful scene the end of the dynasty of Peter the Great? And was this the end of Catherine's aspirations? The empress was anxious to avoid infecting the girl before the wedding, so Catherine, at her request, set out again for St. Petersburg with her mother, leaving Her Majesty at the Grand Duke's bedside.

For weeks, in a primitive and poorly heated hovel, Elizabeth watched over the stupid and ungrateful heir who had played such a nasty trick, trying to back out of the game just when they were both on the point of winning. And little by little, Peter's fever diminished and he began to achieve some relative lucidity.

By the end of January 1745, Peter had recovered from the fever and the empress escorted him back to St. Petersburg. He had changed so much during his illness that Elizabeth was afraid the bride-to-be would be shocked — her fiancé, never handsome, was now revolting. The small pox had disfigured him terribly. With his shaved head, swollen face, bloodshot eyes and cracked lips, he was a caricature of the young man he had been just a few months before. Catherine was sure to be horrified. Elizabeth put a big wig on Peter's head in an attempt to improve his disastrous appearance, but topped with a cascade of false curls, he looked even worse. There wasn't much to do but allow destiny take its course. As soon as the travelers had arrived and settled into the Winter Palace, young Catherine rushed to visit her miraculously recuperated fiancé. Elizabeth, heart in throat, presided over their reunion. At the sight of Grand Duke Peter, Catherine froze. Her mouth half-opened, her eyes wide, she stammered out some pleasantry to congratulate her fiancé on his recovery, dropped a quick curtsey and fled as if she had just met a ghost.

February 10 was the Grand Duke's birthday. The empress, dismayed by his appearance, even advised him against showing himself in public. However, she still harbored the hope that, over time, his physical flaws would begin to fade. What concerned her more, for the time being, was the little interest he showed in his betrothed. According to people in Catherine's entourage, Peter had boasted to her of having had mistresses. But was he even capable of satisfying a woman? Was he "normal," in that regard? And would the delightful Catherine be charming enough, inventive enough to awaken the desire of such an odd husband? Would she give children to the country that was already impatient for them? What could remedy the sexual deficiency of a man who found the sight of a well-trained regiment more exciting than that of a young woman lying languidly in the shadows of the bedroom? The doctors, taking secret council, decided that the Grand Duke might find the ladies more attractive if he drank less. Moreover, in their opinion, his inhibition was only temporary and he would

soon go through a "better phase." Lestocq concurred. But the empress was surprised that neither Catherine nor Peter was in any
hurry. After lengthy discussions, she set the date of the ceremony,
irrevocably. The most superb weddings of the century would take
place on August 21, 1745.

Footnotes

1. Catherine II : *Mémoires*.
2. A pejorative name signifying "Razumovsky's mother".
3. K. Waliszewski, *op. cit.*
4. Reported by K. Waliszewski : *La Dernière des Romanov, Élisabeth Ire*.
5. Cf. Daria Olivier, *op. cit.*

IX

Elizabethan Russia

When it came to organizing these important festivities, Elizabeth left nothing to chance. The morning of the ceremony, she sat in Catherine's dressing room and examined her, naked, from head to toe. She directed the maids-in-waiting in the selection of underclothes, discussed with the hairdresser the best way of arranging her hair, and chose, unilaterally, the silver brocaded gown with a full skirt, short sleeves, and a train embroidered with roses. Then, emptying her jewel case, she supplemented the ornamentation with necklaces, bracelets, rings, brooches and elaborate earrings, all of which so weighed down the bride that she was reduced to posing like a hieratic figure, barely able to move. The grand duke, too, was encased in silver fabric and decked out in imperial jewels; but while the bride may have appeared like a celestial vision, he, looking like a monkey disguised as a prince, was liable to provoke a good laugh. The buffoons that had surrounded Her Majesty Anna Ivanovna were never so funny (when they tried to be) as he was when trying to look serious.

The procession traversed St. Petersburg amid a multitude of

spectators who prostrated themselves as the carriages went by, making the sign of the cross and calling out their blessings and good wishes for the young couple and the tsarina. Never did so many candles glow in the Cathedral of Our Lady of Kazan. Throughout the liturgy, Elizabeth was on the lookout for one of her nephew's little stunts, having come to expect some disruption from him during the most serious occasions. But the service went off without a hitch, including the exchange of rings. After risking ankylosis by standing upright throughout the service, the assembly then flexed its legs at the ball that, of course, capped the day's festivities.

However, no matter how much she enjoyed dancing, Elizabeth kept her mind on the essential matter — which was not the Church blessing, and far less the minuets and the polonaises, but the coupling which, in theory, should soon take place. By 9:00 in the evening, she decided that it was time for the young couple to withdraw. As a conscientious duenna, she led them to the bridal apartment. The matrons and maids of honor, all a-twitter, gave them escort. The grand duke discreetly disappeared to don his night clothes. The grand duchess's maidservants took advantage of the husband's absence to dress the young lady in a chemise that was tantalizingly transparent, and capped her hair with a light bonnet of lace; she was put to bed under the vigilant eye of the empress. When Her Majesty judged that "the little one" was "ready," she exited — with theatrical slowness. She would have loved dearly to be able to see what happened next. Would her wretched nephew be able to summon up enough manhood to satisfy this poor young girl? Wouldn't they need her helpful advice? Catherine looked frightened and had tears in her eyes — a virginal apprehension that must only excite the desire of a normally constituted man. But how would the eccentric grand duke behave? Might he not harbor an impotence that no woman could cure?

In the days that followed, she studied Catherine, vainly look-ing for signs of conjugal satisfaction. The bride appeared increas-ingly thoughtful and disillusioned. Questioning her chamber-maids, Elizabeth learned that, every evening, after having joined his wife in bed, instead of cherishing her, the grand duke would amuse himself with the wooden figurines on his bedside table. And often, they said, he would abandon the grand duchess on the pretext of a headache to go have a drink and a laugh with some of his friends in a nearby room. Sometimes he even played with the servants, ordering them about as if they were soldiers on parade. These may all have been harmless infantile pleasures, but they must have been offensive, and worrisome, for a wife who was only waiting to be undressed.

Catherine may have been languishing untouched at the side of a husband who shirked his duties; but her mother was carrying on shamelessly. In just a few months in St. Petersburg, she man-aged to become the mistress of Count Ivan Betsky. She was thought to be pregnant by him, and people were saying that even if the grand duchess should be long in giving the empire an heir, her dear mother would soon be presenting her with a little brother or sister. Offended by the misconduct of this woman who, out of regard for Catherine, should have moderated her pas-sions during her stay in Russia, Elizabeth firmly invited her to leave the country where she had exhibited only dishonor and stu-pidity. After a pathetic scene, with excuses and justifications on one side and icy contempt on the other, Johanna packed her bags and returned to Zerbst without saying good-bye to her daughter, who was sure to have reproached her.

Although having been dismayed by her mother's extrava-gances all this time, Catherine felt so alone after Johanna's depar-ture that her melancholy transformed into a quiet despair. Wit-nessing this collapse, Elizabeth still struggled to believe that upon seeing how unhappy his wife had become, Peter would draw closer to Catherine and that her tears would succeed where ordinary coquetry had failed. But, from one day to the next, the lack of understanding between the spouses grew deeper. Upset by his inability to fulfill his marital duty, as Catherine invited him to do every night with a sweetly provocative smile, he took revenge by claiming — with all the cynicism of an army grunt — that he had other women, and that he even had a strong attachment elsewhere. He told her that he had something going on with some of her ladies-in-waiting, who supposedly held him in great affection. In his desire to humiliate Catherine, he went as far as scoffing at her subservience towards the Orthodox religion and for her respect for the empress, that hoyden who was openly flaunting her relations with the ex-*muzhik* Razumovsky. Her Majesty's turpitude was, he said, the talk of the town.

Elizabeth would have been merely amused by the trouble in the Grand-Ducal household if her daughter-in-law had quit brooding for long enough to find a way to get pregnant. But, after nine months of cohabitation, the young woman was as flat in the belly as she had been on her wedding day. Could she still be a virgin? This prolonged sterility seemed like an attack on Elizabeth's personal prestige. In a fit of anger, she called in her unproductive daughter-in-law, said that she alone was responsible for the non-consummation of the marriage, accused her of frigidity, clumsiness and (following suit from the chancellor, Alexis Bestuzhev) went as far as to claim that Catherine shared her mother's political convictions and must be working secretly for the king of Prussia.

The grand duchess protested, in vain. Elizabeth announced that, from now on, the grand duke and she would have to shape up. Their lives, intimate as well as public, would now be subject to strict rules in the form of written "instructions" from Chancel-

lor Bestuzhev, and the execution of this program would be ensured by "two people of distinction": a master and a mistress of
the court, to be named by Her Majesty. The master of the court
would be charged with instructing Peter in propriety, correct language and the healthy ideas that were appropriate to his station;
the mistress of the court would encourage Catherine to adhere to
the dogmas of the Orthodox religion under every circumstance;
she would keep her from making the least intrusion in the field of
politics, would keep away from her any young men liable to distract her from her marital commitment, and would teach her certain feminine wiles that might enable her to awaken the desire of
her husband, so that, as one reads in the document, "by this means
our very high house may produce offspring."[1]

Pursuant to these draconian directives, Catherine was forbidden to write directly to anyone. All her correspondence, including letters to her parents, would be subjected to review by the
College of Foreign Affairs. At the same time, the few gentlemen
whose company sometimes distracted her in her loneliness and
sorrow were removed from the court. Thus, by order of Her Majesty, three Chernyshevs (two brothers and a cousin, all good-
looking and pleasant of address) were sent to serve as lieutenants
in regiments cantoned in Orenburg. The mistress of the court,
responsible for keeping Catherine in line, was a German cousin of
the empress, Maria Choglokov, and the master of the court was
none other than her husband, an influential man currently on a
mission in Vienna. This model household was intended to serve
as an example to the ducal couple. Maria Choglokov was a paragon of virtue, since she was devoted to her husband, appeared to
be pious, viewed every issue from the same perspective as Bestuzhev — and at the age of 24 already had four children! If need be,
the Choglokovs might be backed up by an additional mentor,
Prince Repnin, who would also be charged with imbuing Their

Highnesses with wisdom and a preference for all things Russian, including the Orthodox faith.

With such assets working in her favor, Elizabeth was sure she would breach the divide in this household; but she very soon saw that it is as difficult to engender reciprocal love in a disparate couple as it is to institute peace between two countries with opposing interests. In the world at large as in her own house, misunderstanding, rivalry, demands, confrontations and rifts were the rule.

From threats of war to local skirmishes, from broken treaties to troop concentrations at the borders, it happened that, after the French armies enjoyed a few victories in the United Provinces, that Elizabeth agreed to send expeditionary forces to the borders of Alsace. Without actually engaging in hostilities with France, she wanted to encourage it to show a little more flexibility in negotiating with its adversaries. On October 30, 1748, through the peace treaty of Aachen, Louis XV gave up the conquest of the Netherlands and Frederick II retained Silesia. The tsarina left the field, having gained nothing and lost nothing, but having disappointed everyone. The only sovereign who was pleased with this result was the king of Prussia.

By now, Elizabeth was convinced that Frederick II was entertaining in St. Petersburg, within the very walls of the palace, one of his most effective and most dangerous partisans: the Grand Duke Peter. Her nephew, whom she never could stand, was becoming more foreign and more odious by the day. To cleanse the atmosphere of Germanophilia in which the grand duke was submerged, she set out to eliminate from his retinue all the gentlemen from Holstein, and to remove the others who might try to replace them. Even Peter's manservant, a certain Rombach, was thrown into prison on a trumped up pretext.

Peter comforted himself after these affronts by indulging in extravagant whims. He began playing his violin ceaselessly, scraping away for hours, tormenting his wife. His rhetoric became so bizarre that sometimes Catherine thought he'd gone mad; she wanted to flee. Whenever he saw her reading, he would rip the book from her hands and order her to join him in playing with his collection of wooden soldiers. Having recently developed a passion for dogs, he moved ten barbet spaniels into the marital bedroom, over Catherine's protests. When she complained about their barking and their odor, he insulted her and refused to sacrifice his pack for her.

Isolated, Catherine sought in vain for a friend or, at least, a confidant. She finally turned Lestocq, the empress's doctor, secure in his tenure, who showed some interest and even sympathy for Catherine. She hoped to make him an ally against the "Prussian clique" as well as against Her Majesty, who was still reproaching her for the sterility that was beyond her control. Unable to correspond freely with her mother, she asked the doctor to see her letters on their way, more privately. However Bestuzhev, who hated Lestocq and saw him as a potential rival, was delighted to hear from his spies that the "quack" was flouting the imperial instructions and rendering services to the grand duchess. Backed by these revelations, he contacted Razumovsky and accused Lestocq of being an agent in the pay of foreign chancelleries; and he said that Lestocq was trying to take the shine off the favorite's reputation with Her Majesty. This denouncement agreed with denunciations made by a secretary to the doctor, a certain Chapuzot who, under torture, acknowledged everything that he was asked. Confronted with this sheaf of more or less convincing evidence, Elizabeth was put on her guard. For several months already, she had avoided being under Lestocq's care; if he was no longer reliable, he would have to pay.

In the night of November 11, 1748, Lestocq was yanked from

his bed and thrown into a cell in the Peter and Paul Fortress. A special commission, chaired by Bestuzhev in person, with General Apraxin and Count Alexander Shuvalov as assessors, accused Lestocq of having sold out to Sweden and Prussia, of corresponding clandestinely with Johanna of Anhalt-Zerbst, mother of the Grand Duchess Catherine, and of conspiring against the empress of Russia. After being tortured, and despite his oaths of innocence, he was shipped off to Uglich, and stripped of all his possessions.

However, in a reflex of tolerance, Elizabeth granted that the condemned man's wife could join him in his cell and, later, in exile. Perhaps she felt sorry for the fate of this man whom she had to punish, on royal principle, event though she had such positive memories of the eagerness with which he had always offered his services. Elizabeth may not have been good, but she was sensitive, and even sentimental. Incapable of granting clemency, she nonetheless had always been willing to shed tears for the victims of an epidemic in some remote country or for the poor soldiers who were risking their lives at the borders of the realm. Since she was usually presented to her subjects in a familiar and smiling guise, they, forgetting the torments, spoliations, and executions ordered under her reign, called her "The Lenient." Even her ladies of honor, whom she sometimes thanked with a good hard slap or an insult harsh enough to make a soldier blush, would melt when, having wrongfully punished them, she would admit her fault. But it was with her morganatic husband, Razumovsky, that she showed her most affectionate and most attentive side. When the weather was cold, she would button his fur-lined coat, taking care that this gesture of marital solicitude was seen by all their entourage. Whenever he was confined to his armchair by a bout of gout — as often happened— she would sacrifice important appointments to bear him company, and life at the palace would return to normal only after the patient had recovered.

However, she did allow herself to deceive him with vigorous young men like the counts Nikita Panin and Sergei Saltykov. But, of all her secondary lovers, her favorite was Shuvalov's nephew, Ivan Ivanovich. She was attracted by this new recruit's alluring youth and good looks, but also by his education and his knowledge of France. She, who never spent a minute reading, was filled with wonder to see him so impatient to receive the latest books that were being sent to him from Paris. At the age of 23, he was corresponding with Voltaire! With him, one could abandon oneself to love and culture, both at the same time — and without even tiring the eyes and taxing the brain! Certainly, being introduced to the splendors of art, literature, and science in the arms of a man who was a living encyclopedia must be one of the pleasantest methods of education. Elizabeth seemed to be so happy with this arrangement that Razumovsky did not even think of reproaching her for this betrayal. He even considered Ivan Shuvalov worthy of esteem and encouraged Her Majesty to pursue her pleasure and her studies with him.

With Ivan Shuvalov's encouragement, Elizabeth founded the University of Moscow and the Academy of Fine Arts in St. Petersburg. Aware of her own ignorance, she must have enjoyed the irony and felt proud to preside over the awakening of the intellectual movement in Russia, and to know that the writers and the artists of tomorrow would be so much in her debt, despite her lack of learning.

However, while Razumovsky wisely allowed himself to be supplanted by Ivan Shuvalov in Her Majesty's good graces, Chancellor Bestuzhev guessed that his own preeminence was threatened by this rising scion of a large and ambitious clan. He tried hard to distract the tsarina with the charming Nikita Beketov; but, after having dazzled Her Majesty during a show put on by the students in the Cadet Academy, this Adonis was called up to serve in the army. He was brought back to St. Petersburg, where he could again be placed before Her Majesty, but it was no use. The Shuvalov clan made short work of him. Out of pure friendship, they recommended a certain face cream to him; and, when Beketov tried it, red spots broke out on his face and he was smitten with a high fever. In his delusion, he made indecent comments about Her Majesty. He was driven out the palace and never managed to set foot there again, leaving the way clear for Ivan Shuvalov and Alexis Razumovsky, who both accepted and respected each other.

Under their combined influence, the tsarina gave way to her passion for building, seeking to prove herself a worthy heir to Peter the Great by embellishing his city, St. Petersburg. She spared no expense in renovating the Winter Palace, and in three years she had a summer palace built at Tsarskoye Selo, which would become her favorite residence. The chief architect of all these enormous projects, the Italian Bartolomeo Francesco Rastrelli, also erected a church at Peterhof and designed the park surrounding the palace, as well as the gardens of Tsarskoye Selo. To compete with Louis XV (whom she took as her model in the art of royal ostentation), Elizabeth turned to the highly regarded European painters of the day, commissioning them to bequeath to the curiosity of the future generations the portraits of Her Majesty and her close friends. After the court painter Caravaque, she invited the very famous Jean-Marc Nattier to come from France. But he changed his mind at the last minute, and she had to settle for his son-in-law, Louis Tocqué, who was won over by an offer of 26,000 rubles from Ivan Shuvalov. In two years, Tocqué painted ten canvases and, at the end of his contract, passed the brush to Louis-Joseph Le Lorraine and to Louis-Jean-François Lagrenée.[2] All these artists were chosen, advised and appointed by Ivan Shu-

valov — he performed his best services for the glory of his imperial mistress by attracting to St. Petersburg such talented foreign
painters and architects.

Elizabeth felt it was her duty to enrich the capital with
beautiful buildings and to embellish the royal apartments with
paintings worthy of the galleries of Versailles; at the same time,
she had the ambition (although she seldom opened a book) to ini-
tiate her compatriots to the delights of the mind. She spoke
French rather well and even tried to write verse in that language
(as was the rage in all the European courts), but it soon became
clear that that pastime was beyond her abilities. On the other
hand, she encouraged a proliferation of ballet performances, on
the premise that such shows are, at least, an amusing way to participate in the general culture. Most of the ballets were directed
by her dance master, Landet. Even more than these theatrical eve-
nings, the innumerable balls served as an occasion for the women
to exhibit their most elegant ensembles. But, at these gatherings,
they hardly spoke — neither among themselves nor with the male
guests. Social mores were still exceedingly conservative; indeed,
mixed-gender events were still something of a novelty in this
God-fearing world. The ladies, mute and stiff, would line up along
one side of the room, their eyes lowered, not looking at the gentlemen aligned on the other side. Later on, the swirling couples also
displayed a numbing decency and slowness. "The repetitious and
always uniform attendance of these pleasures quickly becomes
tiresome," would write the sharp-tongued Chevalier d'Éon. Similarly, the Marquis de l'Hôpital told his minister, the duke of
Choiseul: "I won't even mention the boredom; it is inexpressible!"

Elizabeth tried to shake some life into these events by en-
couraging the first theater performances in the history of Russia.
She authorized the installation of a company of French actors in
St. Petersburg, while the Senate granted the Hilferding Germans

the privilege of staging comedies and operas in both capitals. Moreover, Russian popular shows began to be offered to the public on feast days in St. Petersburg and Moscow. Among others, *The Mystery of the Nativity* was staged; however, out of respect for Orthodox dogmas, Elizabeth prohibited anyone from impersonating the Blessed Virgin; thus, instead of having an actress play that role, an icon would be brought on stage whenever the play called for the mother of God to speak. Moreover, a law enforced by the police prevented any plays (even those of religious inspiration) from being produced in private residences.

At around this time a young author, Alexander Sumarokov, created a hit with a tragedy written in the Russian language: *Khorev*. And a 1000-seat theater, considered an incredible innovation, was built in Yaroslavl, in the provinces. It was founded by a certain Fyodor Grigorievich Volkov, who put on plays that he had composed, in prose and in verse. Often, he acted in them himself. Astonished by the Russian elite's sudden passion for the theater, Elizabeth took her benevolence as far as authorizing actors to bear swords, an honor previously reserved for the nobility.

For the most part, the plays presented in St. Petersburg and Moscow were pallid Russian adaptations of the most renowned French plays. Molière's *The Miser* and *Tartuffe* and Corneille's *Polyeucte* were favorites. Suddenly, struck by a flash of inspiration, Sumarokov wrote a Russian historical drama, *Sinav and Truvor*, based on the history of the republic of Novgorod. This experiment in national literature made it all the way to Paris, where its novelty was hailed as a curiosity in *Le Mercure de France*. Little by little the Russian public, impelled by Elizabeth and Ivan Shuvalov, became interested in this new form of expression; while it began as an imitation of the great *œuvres* of Western literature, when rendered in the mother tongue it acquired a semblance of originality. Sumarokov was on a trajectory; he launched a literary review, *The Busy Bee*, which evolved in a year's time into a weekly magazine, *Leisure*, published by the Cadet Corps. He even enlivened the texts with a bit of irony, in the style of Voltaire but devoid of the least philosophical provocation. In short, he was a whirlwind, stirring up something new every day in this virgin field. And still, he and other pioneers as talented as Trediakov and Kantemir were bested by yet another author who had sprung to prominence. And in this case, too, it was Shuvalov who "discovered" the genius in that odd character, part intellectual, part Jack-of-all-trades, part vagabond, that was Sergei Lomonosov.

Son of a humble fisherman in the Arkhangelsk region, Lomonosov spent most of his childhood on his father's boat, on the cold and stormy waters between the White Sea and the Atlantic Ocean. A parish priest taught him to read and, inspired by an abrupt passion for scholarship and for wandering, he fled the family home and set off on foot, ragged and famished, sleeping anywhere he could, eating anything he could find, living on charity and thievery but never deviating from his goal: Moscow. He was 17 years old when he finally arrived, with his belly empty and his head full of dazzling plans. Picked up by a monk, he presented himself as the son of a priest who had come to study under the great minds of the city; and lo and behold, he was admitted, as the monk's protégé, to the Slavo-Greco-Latin Academy (the only educational institution then in existence in the Russian empire). He was quickly noted there for his exceptional intelligence and sharp memory, on the basis of which he was sent to St. Petersburg and from thence to Germany. His principals instructed him to complete his knowledge in all areas. In Marburg, the philosopher and mathematician Christian von Wolff befriended him, encouraged him in his readings, introduced him to the works Descartes and to intellectual debate.

But, while Lomonosov was attracted by intellectual specula-
tion, he also enjoyed poetry, especially since in Germany, under
the aegis of Frederick II (who had a passion for culture), versifica-
tion was a very fashionable pastime. Exalted by the examples
from above, Lomonosov wrote verse too, plentifully and quickly.
However, these literary exercises did not keep him pinned behind
his desk for too long. All of a sudden he dropped his studies and
started frequenting gambling dens and chasing skirts. His conduct was so scandalous that he was threatened with arrest, and
had to leave the country lest he be forcibly enrolled in the Prussian army. He was caught and imprisoned but managed to escape
and, out of money and out of energy, made it back to St. Petersburg.

These successive adventures, far from persuading him to
conform, made him resolve to fight with all his strength against
bad fate and false friends. Nevertheless, this time he sought to
distinguish himself by producing poetry rather than by consum-
ing alcohol. His admiration for the tsarina inspired him; he saw in
her not only the heiress of Peter the Great, but the symbol of Russia moving toward a glorious future. In a beautiful burst of sincerity, he dedicated poems of almost religious reverence to Her Majesty. Certainly, he was well aware that in this, he was following
in the footsteps of Vasily Trediakovsky and Alexander Sumarokov, but these two colleagues (who hardly welcomed his advent
in the tight intellectual circles of the capital) did not intimidate
him in the least. He and they both knew that he would soon cast
them into the shade with the brilliance and scope of his visions
and his vocabulary. He was hunting on the same grounds as they.
Following their example, he penned panegyrics to Her Majesty
and anthems to the military prowess of Russia. But, while the
pretexts of Lomonosov's poems remained conventional, his style
and prosody had a new vigor. His predecessors were mired in the

stilted, pompous conventions of a language that was still impregnated with Old Slavonic. His writings were the first in Russia to approach — timidly, it is true — the language spoken by people who grew up on something other than scriptures and breviaries. Without actually descending from Mount Olympus, he took a few steps toward everyday speech. Who, among his contemporaries, would not find that appealing? He was widely acclaimed. But he was so avid for knowledge that literary success was not enough for him. Pushing the limits of ambition, he strove to cover the entire spectrum of human thought, to learn everything, to experience everything, and to succeed at everything all at the same time.

He was supported by Ivan Shuvalov, who had him appointed President of the Academy; he inaugurated his role by establishing a course in experimental physics. His curiosity encompassed every discipline, so that he published, one after another, an *Introduction to the True Physical Chemistry*, a *Dissertation on the Duties of Journalists in the Essays They Write on the Freedom to Philosophize* (in French) and, probably to bolster his reputation among the Orthodox clergy, suspicious as they were of Western atheism, a *Reflection on the Utility of Ecclesiastical Books in the Russian Language*. Many other works flowed from his prolific pen — including odes, epistles, and tragedies. In 1748, he composed a treatise on rhetoric, in Russian. The following year, he set out to make an in-depth study on the industrial coloring of glass; and with the same enthusiasm, he undertook to draft the first lexicon of the Russian language. By turns poet, chemist, mineralogist, linguist, and grammarian, he would spend weeks at a time cloistered in his office in St. Petersburg or at the laboratory that he had set up in Moscow, in the Sukharev Tower, built by Peter the Great. Rather than wasting time eating, when so many pressing problems needed his attention, he would gulp down a few slices of buttered bread and a beer or two, and go on working until he fell asleep in his chair. As the night deepened, passersby would be worried by the light that still shone in his window — they wondered whether his labors were inspired by the God or the Devil. A monster of scholarship and intellectual avidity, warring against the ignorance and fanaticism of the people, Lomonosov even claimed, in 1753, to have preceded Benjamin Franklin in discovering electricity. But he was also concerned with the practical applications of science and so, still with the support of Shuvalov, he reorganized the first university, built an imperial porcelain factory, and established the art of glassmaking and mosaics in Russia.

Having very quickly recognized Lomonosov's merits, Elizabeth repaid him in admiration and protection for the homage that he dedicated to her in his poems. She may have been only semi-illiterate, but her instincts sometimes filled in where culture was lacking. It was that same instinct that had led her to choose as her lover, then as *de facto* husband, a simple peasant and former church cantor, and to entrust the education of her empire to another peasant, the son of a fisherman — a genius and a polygraph. In both cases, she resorted to a child of the people to help her raise the people. In the end, the most significant legacy of her reign would be neither the monuments nor the laws, the ministers appointed or the battles won, nor all the festivals and fireworks, but the birth of the true Russian language. Nobody around her had yet sensed that, beneath the superficial calm, the country was undergoing a revolution. Not only were the mindsets and the morals changing imperceptibly, but the way in which people were choosing and arranging words to express their thoughts. Freed from the ancestral yoke of Church Slavonic, the Russian language of the future was beginning to take shape. And was the son of a fisherman from the Far North who, through his writings, was making the nobility literate.

Lomonosov's greatest stroke of fortune was to have Elizabeth to help him in his extraordinary career; and Elizabeth's greatest stroke of fortune was in having Lomonosov to create, under her wing, the Russian language of the future.

Footnotes

1. Cf. Henri Troyat: *Catherine la Grande*, and Bilbassov: *Catherine II.*
2. Cf. Daria Olivier, *op. cit.*

X

Her Majesty and Their Imperial Highnesses

1750 was a difficult year. Pulled in every direction, by world events as well as family affairs, Elizabeth was at her wits' ends. Europe had fallen into a convulsion of competition and conflict, and the grand ducal couple was doing no better; neither drama seemed to have a clear plot or plan for the future.

Peter's coarseness cropped up at every turn. His childish behavior, which should have improved with age, only grew more extreme. At the age of 22, he was still playing with dolls — directing his little band of Holstein soldiers dressed in Prussian uniforms in parades at Oranienbaum, and organizing mock military tribunals to condemn a foot soldier to be hanged. As for the games of love, he made less and less pretense of having any interest. He still boasted in front of Catherine about his alleged affairs, but he made very sure never to touch her. Was he afraid of her, or was she repulsive to him precisely because she was a woman and he was so ignorant about that kind of creature?

Frustrated and humiliated, night after night, she distracted herself with the many-volume French novels of Mlle. de Scudéry,

Honoré d'Urfé's 5000-page pastoral romance *Astrea, Clovis* by Desmarets, Mme. de Sévigné's *Letters* and — what nerve! — *The Lives of Gallant Ladies* by Brantôme. When she was good and tired of turning the pages, she would dress as a man (following the empress's example) and would go out to shoot ducks by the edge of a pond, or have a horse saddled and go off at a gallop, aimlessly racing the wind, struggling to calm her nerves. She was still sufficiently concerned with propriety to start out riding sidesaddle, but as soon as she thought she was out of sight, she would sit astride the horse. Duly informed, the empress deplored this practice which, in her view, might cause sterility in her daughter-in-law. Catherine must have wondered whether to be touched or outraged at this continued interest in her physical condition.

While the grand duke scorned her, other men were now courting her — and more or less openly. Even her appointed mentor, the so-virtuous Choglokov, was charmed by her and would drop a salacious compliment from time to time. Having been pleased by the attentions of the Chernyshevs in earlier days, Catherine now had the pleasure of basking in the assiduous attentions of a new member of the family; his name was Zahar, and he was certainly equal to his predecessors. At every ball Zahar was there, gazing at her with adoration and waiting for his chance to dance with her. There were even rumors that they had exchanged love letters. Elizabeth was afraid they might go too far, and broke up their flirtation. Chernyshev received on imperial order to rejoin his regiment immediately, far from the capital.

But Catherine hardly had time to miss him, for almost at once his place was taken by the seductive count Sergei Saltykov. Descendant of one of the oldest and greatest families of the empire, he was accepted among the chamberlains of the junior court surrounding the grand duke and duchess. He was married to one of the empress's young ladies of honor, and had two children by her. He was thus a member of the race of "real men" and was burning to prove it to the grand duchess, but prudence still held him back. The couple's new monitor and chambermaid, Miss Vladislavov, an assistant to the Choglokovs, kept Bestuzhev and the empress informed of the progress of this doubly adulterous idyll.

One day, while Mrs. Choglokov was explaining to Her Majesty, for the tenth time, her concern about the grand duke's neglect of his wife, Elizabeth finally had an inspiration. As her advisor had just repeated, no child could be born if the husband failed to "have some input." Thus it was on Peter that and not on Catherine that they should be concentrating. Elizabeth summoned Alexis Bestuzhev and went over with him the best ways of solving the problem. The facts were simple: after five years of marriage, the grand duchess had not been deflowered by her husband. However, according to the latest news, she had a lover, a "normal" man, Sergei Saltykov. Consequently, it was essential, to avoid an annoying intrigue, to beat Saltykov to the prize and make it possible for Peter to fertilize his wife. According to Boerhaave, the court doctor, a minor surgical procedure would relieve His Highness of the phimosis that made him unable to satisfy his august bride. Of course, if the operation did not succeed, Sergei Saltykov would be on hand to fulfill the role of sire, *incognito*. Thus they would have a double guarantee of insemination. In other words, to ensure the future lineage of Peter the Great, they had better bet on both horses: by allowing Catherine to enjoy herself with her lover and, at the same time, by preparing her husband to have effective relations with her. Concern for the dynasty and family feeling combined to persuade the tsarina to use every arrow in her quiver. And anyway, not having had a child herself in spite of her many love affairs, she could not imagine why any woman whose physical constitution did not preclude maternity might hesitate to seek with another man the happiness that her husband refused her. Little by little, in her mind, the grand duchess's adultery (which at first seemed only a futile and aberrant idea) became an obsession approaching a holy conviction, the equivalent of a patriotic duty.

Thus at Elizabeth's instigation Mrs. Choglokov, now transformed into a very intimate confidante, was to explain to Catherine that there are situations in which the honor of a woman requires that she agree to lose that honor for the good of the country. She swore to her that nobody — not even the empress — would blame her for transgressing the rules of marital fidelity. And so it was with the blessing of Her Majesty, Bestuzhev and Choglokov that she now found it possible to meet Sergei Saltykov for pleasures that went far beyond flirtatious conversation.

Meanwhile, the minor surgical procedure that those on high had decided should be visited upon the person of the grand duke was effected painlessly. To make sure that this flourish of the scalpel had made her nephew "operational," Her Majesty sent the pretty young widow of the painter Groot to visit him; she was said to very apt at assessing a man's capabilities. The lady's report was conclusive: everything was in working order! The grand duchess would be able to judge for herself the (finally) normal capacities of her husband. Sergei Saltykov was relieved to hear this news; and Catherine was even more so. Indeed, it was high time that Peter should make an appearance, at least once, in her bed so that she could have him endorse the paternity of the child whom she had already been carrying for a few weeks.

Alas! on December 1750, during a shooting party, Catherine was racked with violent pains. A miscarriage. In spite of their disappointment, the tsarina and the Choglokovs redoubled their attentions; one way or another, they invited her to try again — with Saltykov or any other stand-in. At this point, it hardly mattered who the true father might be — it was the putative father that counted! In March 1753, Catherine found herself pregnant again; and suffered a second miscarriage, after a ball. Fortunately, the tsarina was obstinate: instead of despairing, she encouraged Saltykov in his role as stud, so that in February 1754, seven months after her last miscarriage, Catherine noted that she was again showing the hoped-for signs. The tsarina was notified immediately. The pregnancy appeared to be proceeding correctly, and she reckoned that it would be wise to remove Saltykov, whose services were no longer necessary. However, out of regard for her daughter-in-law's morale, the empress decided to keep the lover in reserve, at least until the child was born.

Certainly, looking forward to this birth, Elizabeth regretted that the result would be a bastard who, although titular heir to the crown, would no longer have a single drop of Romanov blood in his veins. But this genealogical fraud (about which no one, of course, would be informed) was better than leaving the throne to the poor Tsarevich Ivan, now 12 years old and imprisoned at Ryazan (and due to be transferred to Schlüsselburg). Pretending to believe that the expected child was the legitimate offspring of Peter, she smothered with attentions the adulterous mother who was now so indispensable. Torn between remorse for pulling off this epic hoax and pride for thus ensuring the continuity of the dynasty, she would have liked to throw stones at the crafty upstart who had made it possible, and who seemed to be manifesting a sensuality, an amorality and an audacity almost equal to her own; but she had to be circumspect, because it would be the historians of tomorrow who would judge her reign. In the eyes of the court, Her Majesty awaited with pious joy to see her so-affectionate daughter-in-law bring into the world the first son of Grand Duke Peter, the providential fruit of a love blessed by the Church. It was not a woman who was to be confined, but all of

Russia that was preparing to bring forth its future emperor.

For weeks, Elizabeth lodged in the apartment next to the chamber where the grand duchess waited for the great moment. One reason she wanted to stay so close to her daughter-in-law was to prevent the enterprising Sergei Saltykov from visiting her too often, which would set tongues wagging. Let Catherine just give birth, and let her present the country with a boy! Day after day, the tsarina made her calculations, questioned the doctors, consulted fortune-tellers and prayed before the icons.

During the night of September 19, 1754, after nine years of marriage, Catherine finally felt the first pains. The empress, Count Alexander Shuvalov and the Grand Duke Peter rushed to join her. At midday on September 20, 1754, seeing the baby, still sticky and smeared with blood, in the hands of the midwife, Elizabeth exulted: praise the Lord, it was a male! She had already chosen his first name: he would be Paul Petrovich (Paul, son of Peter). Washed, wrapped in a blanket, and baptized by Her Majesty's confessor, the newborn baby stayed only a minute in his mother's arms. She barely had time to hold him, to take in his softness and his scent. He belonged not to her, but to all of Russia — or, rather, to the empress!

Leaving behind the exhausted and groaning grand duchess, Elizabeth carried Paul in her arms like a treasure that had been won at great cost. From now on, she would keep him in her private apartments, under her own care; she didn't need Catherine anymore. Having fulfilled her role by giving birth, the grand duchess was of no further interest. She could just as well return to Germany, and no one in the palace would miss her.

The infant did not exhibit any distinctive "family resemblance" at this age; and so much the better. And anyway, whether he took after Catherine's lover or her husband, the result would be the same. From this point forward, the Grand Duke Peter, pretentious monkey that he was, was only taking up space in the palace. He could disappear: the succession was assured!

All over the city, guns thundered in salute and bells rang joyfully. In her room, Catherine was quite abandoned; and not far away, behind the door sat the grand duke, surrounded by the officers of his Holstein regiment, emptying glass after glass to the health of "his son Paul." As for the diplomats, Elizabeth suspected that in their usual caustic way they would have a field day commenting on the strange lineage of the heir to the throne. But she also knew that, even if the professionals were not taken in by this sleight-of-hand, nobody would dare to say out loud that little Paul Petrovich was a bastard and that the Grand Duke Peter was the most glorious cuckold of Russia. And it was that tacit adherence to an untruth, on the part of her contemporaries, that would transform it into certainty for the future generations. And Elizabeth cared above all for the judgment of posterity.

On the occasion of the baptism, Elizabeth decided to demonstrate how pleased she was with the mother by presenting her with a tray of jewels and an treasury order the sum of 100,000 rubles: the purchase price of an authentic heir. Then, considering that she had shown her sufficient solicitude, she ordered (for the sake of decency) Sergei Saltykov dispatched on a mission to Stockholm. He was charged with conveying to the king of Sweden the official announcement of the birth of His Highness Paul Petrovich in St. Petersburg. She didn't hesitate for a moment over the irony of sending the illegitimate father to collect congratulations for the legitimate father of the child. How long would such a mission last? Elizabeth did not specify, and Catherine was desperate. The tsarina had had too many romantic or sensual affairs in her life to wallow in sentiment over those of others.

While Catherine languished in her bed, waiting for the official "churching," Elizabeth hosted receptions, balls and banquets.

There was nonstop celebration at the palace for this event that had been ten years in the making. Finally, on November 1, 1754, forty days after giving birth, protocol required that the grand duchess receive the congratulations of the diplomatic corps and the court. Catherine, semi-recumbent on a ceremonial chaise upholstered in rose-colored velvet and embroidered in silver, received her visitors in a room that was richly furnished and brightly illuminated for the occasion. The tsarina herself came to inspect the rooms before the ceremony. But, immediately after the homage had been paid, she had the superfluous furniture and candelabra removed; at her instructions, the grand ducal couple found themselves back in their usual apartments at the Winter Palace — a subtle message to let Catherine know that her role was over and that, henceforth, reality would take the place of dreams.

Taking no notice of this family fracas, Peter returned to his puerile games and drinking bouts, while the grand duchess had to face the replacement of her former mentor, Choglokov, who had meanwhile passed away. The new "master of the junior court," who seemed to be particularly nosy and meddlesome, was Count Alexander Shuvalov, Ivan's brother. From the first moment, he sought to gain the sympathy of the habitués of the princely household; he cultivated Peter's friendship and applauded his ill-considered passion for Prussia. With his support, the grand duke now let his Germanophilia run wild. He invited more recruits from Holstein and organized a fortified camp (which he gave the Germanic name of Peterstadt), in the park of the palace of Oranienbaum.

While he was thus amusing himself by pretending to be a German officer, commanding German troops on land that he wished were German, Catherine, feeling more forsaken than ever, sank into depression. As she had feared, shortly after she gave birth, Sergei Saltykov was sent first to Sweden, and then as Russia's resident ambassador to Hamburg. Elizabeth may have hated her adoptive son, but she made a point of cutting off all ties between the two lovers. Moreover, she allowed Catherine to see her baby only on an exceptional basis. More than a possessive mother-in-law, she mounted a guard by the cradle and did not tolerate any input from the grand duchess on how the child was to be raised. Elizabeth ousted Catherine entirely from the role of mother, after she had carried Paul in her womb for nine months and gone through the pain of bringing him into the world.

Robbed and discouraged, Catherine turned to books: Tacitus' *Annals*, Montesquieu's *The Spirit of Laws*, and various essays by Voltaire. Cut off from love, she sought to mitigate this lack of human warmth by delving into the realms of philosophy and politics. Attending the salons of the capital, she listened with more attention than before to the conversations, often brilliant, of the diplomats. While her husband was entirely absorbed in military nonsense, she was gaining assurance and a maturity of mind that did not escape those in her entourage. Elizabeth, whose health was declining as that of Catherine was blossoming, became aware of the progressive metamorphosis of her daughter-in-law — but she could not tell whether she should be delighted or upset. Suffering from asthma and dropsy, in her declining years the tsarina clung to the still young and handsome Ivan Shuvalov. He became her principal reason for living and her best adviser. She wondered whether it would not be better if Catherine, like she, had a designated lover who would fulfill her in every sense and keep her from interfering in public affairs.

In 1751, at Pentecost, a new English plenipotentiary arrived in St. Petersburg. His name was Charles Hambury Williams and in his retinue was a bright young Polish aristocrat, Stanislaw August Poniatowski. The 23-year-old Poniatowski was avidly interested in Western culture, had participated in all the European salons, and was personally acquainted with the famous Mme. Geoffrin in Paris and in London enjoyed the friendship of the minister, Horace Walpole. He was said to be fluent in every language, at ease in every milieu and pleasing to every lady.

As soon as they set foot in Russia, Williams set out to use "the Pole" to seduce the grand duchess and make her an ally in the fight he intended to wage against the grand duke's pro-Prussian passion. And the Chancellor, supported by everyone in the "Russian party," was happy to go along with the British ambassador's plans. Having seen which way the wind was blowing, Bestuzhev wanted to see Russia openly aligned with the English in the event of a conflict with Frederick II. According to the rumor mill, Louis XV himself, smelling war, was impatient to re-establish contact with Russia. Day by day, thanks to her conversations with Stanislaw Poniatowski, Catherine became immersed in every aspect of the European chaos, studying international questions while studying the face of the attractive Pole.

But Poniatowski, despite his many social successes, was terribly shy. Quick with words, he was nonetheless paralyzed by the elegance, grace and talented repartee of the grand duchess. It took a nudge from Leon Naryshkin, Sergei Saltykov's cheerful companion in adventure, to push Poniatowski to declare his interest. Miss Vladislavov, Catherine's chambermaid and confidante, facilitated their first meetings at Oranienbaum. Always well-informed about such intrigues, the tsarina soon heard that her daughter-in-law had found a substitute for Saltykov, that her latest lover was Poniatowski and that the lovebirds were together constantly while the husband, indifferent, closed his eyes.

Elizabeth didn't mind that her daughter-in-law was straying, but she did wonder whether there might not be a political motive behind this love affair. It suddenly occurred to her that there were two rival courts in Russia, one centered around Her Majesty and one centered around the grand-ducal couple — and that the interests of these two centers of power were at odds.

To secure the sympathies of "the great court," traditionally Francophile, Louis XV sent to St. Petersburg a high-level emissary, Sir Mackenzie Douglas. A Scotsman by origin, he was a partisan of the Stuarts and had taken refuge in France; he was part of the "parallel cabinet" of Louis the Well-Loved, called "the King's Secret." His purported mission in Russia was to buy furs; meanwhile, he took the opportunity to communicate to the tsarina a confidential code that would enable her to correspond directly with Louis XV. Before he even started out, Douglas had been informed that his mission had become more delicate than envisaged, for Bestuzhev was now in the pay of London and was serving the British cause. Even the grand duchess, supported by her current lover, was said to be inclined in favor of the English. And Poniatowski, during his temporary absence from the Polish court, had just been granted a prominent official position: he was named Minister for the King of Poland in Russia. Thus his presence in the Russian capital was made more reliable, long-term, giving Catherine more confidence in the possibility of a peaceful future for their relationship. She was further comforted by a certain easing of restrictions in her regard on the part of Alexis Bestuzhev. Having joined the chancellor in the pro-England clan, she was less liable to attack. The odious espionage to which she had been submitted, on behalf of the empress, was removed. The only reports Elizabeth now received from Oranienbaum were in regard to the pro-Prussian extravagances of her nephew.

In this atmosphere of reciprocal surveillance, cautious bargaining and courteous deception, a first treaty was concocted in St. Petersburg in an effort to specify how the various powers would respond in the event of a French-English conflict. But suddenly, following secret negotiations, a new accord was signed in Westminster, on January 16, 1756. It stipulated that, in the case of a generalized war, Russia would join France in its fight against England and Prussia. This abrupt inversion of alliances shocked the uninitiated and appalled Elizabeth. Without a doubt, Bestuzhev, better paid by someone else, had sacrificed Russia's honor-bound commitments to Prussia. And Catherine, that hare-brained young lady, apparently was very happy to follow Bestuzhev in this scandalous about-face. She always had shown herself to be too much impressed with the French spirit! Her Majesty's fury was a combination of political frustration and wounded personal pride. She regretted having trusted Bestuzhev to conduct the international talks, when the vice-chancellor, Vorontsov, and the Shuvalov brothers had been advising her to bide her time.

In order to try to limit the damage, she hastily convened a "conference" in February 1756, where Bestuzhev, Vorontsov, the Shuvalov brothers, Prince Trubestkoy, General Alexander Buturlin, General Apraxin and Admiral Golytsin met under her effective presidency. All these minds, working together, would find a way out of this mess — if anyone could! In the worst case they had to decide whether, assuming a confrontation did take place, Russia could accept "subsidies" in exchange for its neutrality. Draped in imperial honor, Elizabeth said no. But then came word that Louis XV was on the verge of signing a pact of reciprocal military assistance with Maria Theresa, in Austria. Bound by its former engagements to Austria, Russia became, at the same time, an ally of France.

Trapped in spite of herself by Louis XV and Maria Theresa, Elizabeth was obliged to take on Frederick II and George II. Should she be pleased or frightened? All around her, the courtiers were divided between national pride, shame at having betrayed their friends of yesterday, and fear that there would be a high price to pay for this unnecessary change of course. Behind closed doors, it was said that the Grand Duchess Catherine, Bestuzhev, and perhaps even the empress had been bribed to launch the country into a useless war.

Indifferent to these rumors, Elizabeth was astonished to find herself in the position of an unalienable friend of France. Standing tall in the face of misfortune, she hosted a reception on May 7 in honor of Mackenzie Douglas (who was back in St. Petersburg after a brief diplomatic eclipse), and acknowledged him with attention, respect and promises. A few days later, the rather weird Charles de Beaumont (called the Chevalier d'Éon de Beaumont) arrived. This ambiguous and seductive character had already made an initial appearance in Russia; he had worn women's clothing at that time. The elegance of his gowns and the brilliance of his conversation had so impressed the empress that she occasionally had invited him to come and "read" to her. However, now the Chevalier d'Éon was parading in front of her in men's clothing. But whether he presented himself in a skirt or in breeches, she still found him brimming with grace and spirit. Which was his real gender? Elizabeth didn't much care — she showed up both ways, herself, at court masquerades! The main thing was that this gentleman embodied French intelligence and taste. He brought with him a personal letter from the Prince de Conti. The cordial terms of the message touched her more surely than the usual flattery from the ambassadors. Without a moment's hesitation, she declared to him: "I do not wish for any third party or any mediators in a meeting with the King [Louis XV]. I ask of him only truthfulness, sincerity and perfect reciprocity in what we decide between us." This was a straightforward and unambiguous declaration: more than a testimony of confidence, it read like an international declaration of love.

Elizabeth would have liked to take some time to savor this

honeymoon with France, but her insomnia and ill-health no longer left her any respite. The repeated bouts of illness made her fear that she might even lose her wits before winning a decisive victory in the war in which she had been involved, against her wishes, by the game of alliances. And here was Frederick II, taking his enemies by surprise and opening hostilities by invading Saxony without notice.[1] The first engagements were to his advantage. Dresden was taken by storm, the Austrians were defeated in Prague, and the Saxons in Pirna. Forced to stand by her Austrian allies, Elizabeth was resigned to intervening. At her command, General Apraxin, appointed Field Marshal, left St. Petersburg and massed his troops in Riga. When Louis XV dispatched the Marquis de l'Hôpital to exhort the tsarina to take action, she entrusted to Mikhail Bestuzhev (the chancellor's conveniently Francophile brother) the task of signing Russia to the treaty of Versailles. This was done on December 31, 1756.

Secretly embarrassed by taking this ostentatious stand, Elizabeth still hoped that the spreading conflict would not set ablaze all of Europe. She was also afraid that Louis XV might be using her in order to secure a rapprochement, no longer provisional but permanent, with Austria. As if to prove her right, in May 1757 Louis XV proclaimed the need to confirm his commitment to Maria Theresa, in a new alliance intended to bar Prussia from possibly compromising the peace in Europe. Elizabeth surmised that, under this generous pretext, the king was dissimulating a more subtle intention. While declaring solidarity with Russia, he most particularly wanted to ensure that Russia would not seek to expand at the expense of its two neighbors, Poland and Sweden, who were traditional allies of France. As long as Louis XV was playing this double game, he could not play squarely with Elizabeth. She would have to keep stringing along the envoys from Versailles. She wondered whether Alexis Bestuzhev, hobbled by his British sympathies, was still qualified to defend the interests of the country. The chancellor, steadfastly proclaiming his patriotism and integrity, would prefer to see an Anglo-Prussian coalition triumph over an Austro-French coalition (thanks in particular to Russia's inaction); but meanwhile, the empress's lover Ivan Shuvalov had never disguised his penchant for France, its literature, its fashions and, far more important, its political interests. Elizabeth was caught as never before in the struggle between her favorite and her chancellor, the inclinations of her heart (which leaned toward Versailles) and the objections of her mind, which stumbled over her obligations to Berlin.

Critical decisions had to be made, but the daily worries and the recrudescence of her illness undermined her physical stamina a little more every day. She sometimes had hallucinations; she moved to a different bed-chamber because she felt threatened by a faceless enemy; she implored the icons to come to her aid; and once, when she blacked out, she had considerable difficulty pulling together her thoughts again after she regained consciousness. Her fatigue was so profound that she would have liked to give up; but circumstances obliged her to go on.

She knew that behind her back they were already murmuring about the question of her successor. If she were suddenly to die the next day, who would receive the crown? According to tradition, her successor could be only her nephew, Peter. But she rankled at the idea that Russia should go to pieces in the hands of that half-mad, malicious maniac, who paraded around from morning to night in a Holstein uniform. It would be better to declare him incompetent, right now, and to designate the grand duke's two-year-old son, Paul Petrovich, as sole heir. However, that would mean offering the role of regent to Catherine, whom Elizabeth hated as much for her good looks as for her youth, intelligence and many intrigues. Moreover, the grand duchess had lately teamed up with Alexis Bestuzhev. Those two would soon make a mess of all her carefully-laid plans.

This prospect profoundly aggravated the tsarina — then, suddenly, she stopped caring. What difference did it make for her to be concerned with the events of the future, since she presumably would not be there anymore to suffer from them? She was unable to make decisions even concerning the immediate future, and put off the tiresome burden of deciding whether to depose her nephew and hand over the reins of power to her grandson and daughter-in-law, or to allow Peter to accede to the highest seat in the land, at great risk to Russia. She rather hoped that events would take care of themselves.

Precisely at that time, Field Marshal Apraxin fortuitously made up his mind (after she had begged him many times to take action) to launch a vast offensive against the Prussians. In July 1757, Russian troops captured Memel and Tilsitt; in August of the same year, they crushed the enemy at Gross Jaegersdorff. These victories reinvigorated Elizabeth and she celebrated with a *Te Deum*, while Catherine, to please her, organized festivities in the gardens of Oranienbaum. The only sad face in this rejoicing nation was the Grand Duke Peter's. Never mind that he was heir to the throne of Russia and that this series of Russian successes should delight him; he could not get over the defeat of his idol, Frederick II.

The devil must have heard his recriminations — at the very moment when the jubilant crowds in St. Petersburg were shouting "On, to Berlin! On, to Berlin!" and demanding that Apraxin continue his conquest until the very destruction of Prussia, news came that transformed the unanimous enthusiasm into utter amazement. Couriers dispatched by the command affirmed that, after a brilliant beginning, the Field Marshal was beating a retreat and that his regiments had abandoned the occupied terrain on the spot, leaving behind equipment, ammunition and weapons. This flight seemed so inexplicable that Elizabeth suspected a plot. The Marquis de l'Hôpital, who (at the request of Louis XV) was assisting the tsarina to formulate her opinions in these difficult moments, was not far from thinking that the surprising defection of the Field Marshal might not be news to Alexis Bestuzhev and the Grand Duchess Catherine, both in the pay of England and favorable to Prussia.

The ambassador made comments to that effect, and his remarks were reported at once to the tsarina. In a burst of energy, she set out to punish the culprits. To begin with, she recalled Apraxin and assigned him to house arrest, naming his second lieutenant, Count Fermor, to head the army. However, she reserved her principal resentment for Catherine. She would like to prevail, once and for all, against that woman whose marital infidelities she once had tolerated but whose political scheming was beyond the pale. Elizabeth should put an end to her meddling and to all the nonsense kicked up by the comical Prussian clique that was gathered around the grand-ducal couple at Oranienbaum.

Too bad — this was not the time to strike. Catherine was pregnant again, and therefore "sacred" in the eyes of the nation. She was off limits, for the time being. Whatever her flaws, it was better to leave her in peace until she gave birth. And again, who was the father? Surely not the grand duke who, since his little operation, had reserved all his attentions for Elizabeth Vorontsov, the niece of the Vice Chancellor. This mistress, who was neither beautiful nor spiritual, but whose vulgarity was reassuring to him, completely took his mind off his wife. And he didn't care one bit that his wife had a lover, and that it was he who had made her pregnant. He even joked about it, in public. Catherine was nothing to him now but an annoying woman who brought him dishonor, to whom he had been married in his youth, without anyone asking his opinion. He put up with her and tried to stay away from her during the day — and especially at night. She, for her part, feared that Poniatowski, the child's natural father, would be dispatched to the end of the world by the tsarina. At her request, Alexis Bestuzhev interceded with Her Majesty to persuade her to delay Poniatowski's "new assignment" (to Poland) until the birth of the child. He managed to convince her; and Catherine, relaxed, prepared for the event.

Significant contractions gripped her during the night of December 18, 1758. Alerted by her groans, the grand duke was first at her bedside. He was dressed in a Prussian uniform, with boots and sword, spurs at the heels and a commander's sash across his chest. Staggering and mumbling, he declared in a wine-soaked voice that he had come with his regiment to defend his legitimate wife against the enemies of the fatherland. He quickly departed, not wishing to have the Empress discover him in such a state, and went off to ferment in his alcohol. Her Majesty arrived soon after, just in time to see her daughter-in-law delivered by the midwife. Taking the baby in her arms, she examined it like a connoisseur. It was a girl. Too bad — they would have to make do. This was not the end of the world, since the succession was ensured by little Paul. Catherine, seeking to sweeten up her mother-in-law, proposed naming her daughter Elizabeth. But Her Majesty was in no humor for flattery. She said that she preferred to name the child the child Anna, after her elder sister and the grand duke's mother. Then, having had the baby baptized, she savagely took it away, as she had done four years earlier with the brother of this useless infant.

Having gotten past this family episode, Elizabeth devoted herself to settling the Apraxin affair. The Field Marshal, discredited and dismissed after his incomprehensible reversal vis-à-vis the Prussian army that he had just conquered, was struck by a

severe attack of "apoplexy" just at the conclusion of his first interrogation. Before dying, and while denying his culpability, he admitted having corresponded with the grand duchess, Catherine.
However, Elizabeth had formally forbidden her daughter-in-law
from writing to anyone without informing those who were
charged with keeping watch over her; this was, therefore, an un-
forgivable crime of rebellion.

Those close to the tsarina stoked her suspicions against the
grand duchess, Chancellor Alexis Bestuzhev and even Stanislaw
Poniatowski, who were all suspected of intelligence on behalf of
Prussia. Vice Chancellor Vorontsov, whose niece was the grand
duke's mistress and who, for a long time, had dreamed of replacing Bestuzhev, singled out Catherine — he blamed her for all of
Russia's diplomatic and military misfortunes. He constantly at-
tacked the Shuvalov brothers (whose nephew Ivan was Elizabeth's favorite). Even the ambassador of Austria, Count Esterhazy, and the ambassador of France, the Marquis de l'Hôpital,
supported the denigration campaign against Alexis Bestuzhev.
How could the tsarina fail to be impressed by such eager denunciations? After having listened to this concert of reproaches,
Elizabeth made her decision.

One day in February 1759, while Bestuzhev was attending a
ministerial briefing, he was accosted and arrested without explanation. During a searching of his residence, investigators discovered some letters from the grand duchess and Stanislaw Poniatowski. Nothing compromising, certainly; however, in this climate of obscure revenge, the pettiest evidence was sufficient for
settling scores. Of course, in every country, anyone who meddles
in high politics runs the risk of being cast down as quickly as he
may have risen to the top. But, among the so-called civilized na-
tions, the risks are limited to a reprimand, dismissal or early retirement; in Russia, the land of disproportion, culprits could be

would not be such a cad!

It is true that the king of Prussia was counting on the grand duke to bring Russia back to its senses. Elizabeth would prefer to be damned by the Church than to accept such a humiliation! To prove that she was still in charge, on November 17 she took measures to reduce the very unpopular tax on salt and, in a belated burst of leniency, she published a list of prisoners condemned for life whom she suggested should be released. A short time later a hemorrhage, more violent than usual, curtailed all her activity. With every coughing fit, she vomited blood. The doctors stayed by her bedside now and acknowledged that they had given up all hope.

On December 24, 1761, Elizabeth received extreme unction and summoned up the strength to repeat, after the priest, the words of the prayer for the dying. As she slid toward the great void, she guessed how pathetically agitated must be those, in this world that was receding from her little by little, who would have to carry her out to be buried. It was not she who was dying, but the universe of the others. Having failed to make a decision about her succession, she relied on God to settle Russia's fate after she heaved her last sigh. Didn't He know better than anyone down here what was appropriate for the Russian people? For a few more hours, the tsarina held off the night that was invading her brain. The following day, December 25 — the day Christ was born — at about 3:00 in the afternoon, she ceased breathing and a great calm spread across her, where traces of make-up still remained. She had just reached the age of 53.

When the double doors of the death chamber opened wide, all the courtiers assembled in the waiting room knelt down, crossed themselves and lowered their heads to hear the fateful announcement uttered by old prince Nikita Trubestkoy, Procurator General of the Senate: "Her Imperial Majesty Elizabeth Pet-

condemned to ruin, to exile, torture, even death. Catherine, as soon as she felt the chill air of repression tickling the nape of her neck, burned all her old letters, rough drafts, personal notes, and lists of accounts. She hoped that Bestuzhev had taken the same precautions.

In fact, while the Empress condemned her former chancellor, she also wished that he could get away with nothing more than a serious fright and the loss of some privileges. Was this excess of forgiveness due to her age and fatigue, or to the memories of a life of struggle and vice? She decided that this man, who had worked at her side for so long, merited a half-hearted punishment rather than a crushing conviction. Once more, she would be lauded as "the Lenient." Her moderate action against Bestuzhev was all the more meritorious since the other members of the "Anglo-Prussian plot" appeared to have no excuse at all. She maintained a stony countenance when the Grand Duke Peter threw himself at her feet, swearing that he had had nothing to do with these political shenanigans and that Bestuzhev and Catherine alone were guilty of fraud and treason. Disgusted by the baseness of her nephew, Elizabeth sent him to his apartments, without a word. For her, Peter no longer counted. Or existed.

Her attitude was quite the opposite when it came to the "indescribable" conduct of her daughter-in-law. To clear herself, Catherine sent her a long letter, written in Russian; she confided that she was distraught, protested that she was innocent, and beseeched her to allow her to leave for Germany, to go back to her mother and to pray at her father's graveside (he having recently passed away). The idea of voluntary exile for the grand duchess appeared so absurd and so inappropriate in the current circumstances that Elizabeth did not even reply. She chose to punish Catherine by depriving her of her best chambermaid, Miss Vladislavov. This new blow completely demolished the young woman. Consumed by sorrow and fear, she took to bed and refused any food, claiming to be sick in heart and body; on the verge of inanition, she adamantly refused to be examined by a doctor. She begged the obliging Alexander Shuvalov to call a priest to hear her confession. Father Dubiansky, personal chaplain of the tsarina, was alerted. Having received the grand duchess's confession and contrition, he promised to plead her cause with Her Majesty. In a visit to his Majestic penitent, the priest painted such a picture of her daughter-in-law's pain (a daughter-in-law, after all, who could only be reproached for a maladroit devotion to the cause of the monarchy), that Elizabeth promised to reflect on the case of this strange parishioner. Catherine did not yet dare to expect a return to grace. However, Father Dubiansky must have been persuasive in his intervention for, on April 13, 1759, Alexander Shuvalov went to see Catherine in the room where she lay, wasting away in anguish, and announced to her that Her Majesty would receive her "this very day, at ten o'clock in the evening."

Footnotes

1.   This was the beginning of the Seven Years War.

XI

ANOTHER CATHERINE!

This meeting, as the empress and the grand duchess knew full well, would define their relationship forever. They each prepared carefully, marshaling all their arguments, objections, answers and excuses. Elizabeth was imbued with discretionary power, but she was mindful of the fact that her daughter-in-law was just thirty years old, her skin still smooth and her teeth still intact, giving her the advantage of youth and grace. It infuriated the tsarina to find herself over the age of fifty, fat, and able to attract men only by her title and her authority. Suddenly, the competition between two political characters became a competition between women. Catherine had the benefit of age; Elizabeth had the hierarchical advantage.

In order to mark clearly her superiority over the upstart, the tsarina decided to keep her waiting in the antechamber long enough to fray her nerves and weaken her ability to charm. The audience was set for 10:00 in the evening, on April 13; Elizabeth gave orders to introduce Her Highness into the salon only at 1:30 in the morning. Wishing to have witnesses to the lesson that she proposed to inflict on her daughter-in-law, she asked Alexander Shuvalov, her lover Ivan Shuvalov and even the Grand Duke Peter, the culprit's husband, to hide behind large folding screens. She did not invite Alexis Razumovsky to this strange family event — he was still Her Majesty's designated confidant, Her "sentimental memory," but his star had faded recently and he had to yield place, in "significant ways," to younger, more vigorous newcomers. Thus, "the Catherine-and-Peter issue" was outside his sphere of involvement.

This interview was critical, in Elizabeth's view, and she arranged every detail with the meticulous care of a seasoned impresario. Just a few small candles shone in the half-light, accentuating the nerve-wracking character of the meeting. The empress deposited the exhibits in a gold dish: letters from the grand duchess, confiscated from Apraxin and Bestuzhev. Thus, from the first moment, the schemer would be thrown off balance.[1]

However, nothing went as the empress had planned. As soon as she stepped across the threshold, Catherine fell to her knees, wringing her hands and wailing in her sorrow. Between sobs, she claimed that no one in the court cared for her, nobody understood her, and her husband could do nothing but invent ways of humiliating her in public. She begged Her Majesty to allow her to leave for her home country. The tsarina reminded her that it is a mother's duty to remain at the sides of her children, no matter what — to which Catherine retorted, still weeping and sighing: "My children are in your hands and could not receive better care than that!" Touched at a sensitive point by this recognition of her talents as a teacher and protectress, Elizabeth helped Catherine to her feet and gently reproached her for having forgotten all the marks of interest and even affection that she had once lavished upon her. "God is my witness, how I wept when you on your deathbed," she said. "If I had not loved you, I would not have kept you here. . . . But you are extremely proud! You think that nobody has a better mind than you!" At these words, flouting the instructions he had been given, Peter stepped forward and interjected,

"She is terribly spiteful and incredibly stubborn!"

"You must be speaking about yourself!" retorted Catherine. "I have no problem telling you in front of Her Majesty that I really am malicious with you, who advise me to do things that are wrong, and that I certainly have become stubborn since I see that by being agreeable I only earn your spite!"

Before the discussion degenerated into an everyday domestic conflict, Elizabeth sought to regain control. Confronted by this teary woman, she had almost forgotten that the alleged victim of society was a faithless wife and a conspirator. Now, she went on the attack. Pointing to the letters in the gold dish, she said,

"How dared you to send orders to Field Marshal Apraxin?

"I simply asked him to follow your orders," murmured Catherine.

"Bestuzhev says that there were many more!"

"If Bestuzhev says that, he lies!"

'Well, if he is lying, then I will have him put to torture!" exclaimed Elizabeth, giving her daughter-in-law a fatal glance.

But Catherine did not stumble; indeed, the first *passé d'armes* had boosted her confidence. And it was Elizabeth who suddenly felt ill at ease in this interrogation. To calm herself, she began to pace up and down the length of the room. Peter took advantage of the hiatus to launch out in an enumeration of his wife's misdeeds. Exasperated by the invectives from her little runt of a nephew, the tsarina was tempted to side with her daughter-in-law, whom she had just condemned a few minutes before. Her initial jealousy of the young and attractive creature gave way to a kind of female complicity, over the barrier of the generations. In a moment, she cut Peter short and told him to keep silent. Then, approaching Catherine, she whispered in her ear:

"I still had many things to say to you, but I do not want to make things worse [with your husband] than they already are!"

"And I cannot tell you," answered Catherine, "what an urgent desire I have to open to you my heart and my soul!"[2]

This time, it was the Empress whose eyes were filled with tears. She dismissed Catherine and the grand duke, and sat quietly a long time in front of Alexander Shuvalov, who in his turn came out from behind the folding screen. After a moment, she sent him to the grand duchess with a top secret commission: to urge her not to suffer any longer, pointlessly, for Her Majesty hoped to receive her soon for "a genuinely private conversation."

This private conversation did, indeed, take place, in the greatest secrecy, and allowed the two women finally to explain themselves honestly. Did the empress demand, on that occasion, that Catherine provide full details on her liaisons with Sergei Saltykov and Stanislaw Poniatowski, on the exact parentage of Paul and Anna, on the unofficial household of Peter and the dreadful young Vorontsov, on Bestuzhev's treason, Apraxin's incompetence? In any event, Catherine found answers that alleviated Elizabeth's anger, for the very next day she authorized her daughter-in-law to come to see her children in the imperial wing of the palace. During these wisely spaced visits, Catherine was able to observe how well-raised and well-educated were the cherubim, far from their parents.

With the help of these compromises, the grand duchess gave up her desperate plan to leave St. Petersburg to return to her family in Zerbst. Bestuzhev's trial ended inconclusively, because of the lack of material evidence and the death of the principal witness, the Field Marshal Apraxin. Since, in spite of everything, some punishment must be given after so many abominable crimes had been announced, Alexis Bestuzhev was exiled — not to Siberia, but to his own lands, where he would not want for anything.

The principal winner at the end of this legal struggle was Mikhail Vorontsov, who was offered the title of chancellor, replacing the disgraced Bestuzhev. Behind his back, the duke of Choiseul, Secretary of State for Foreign Affairs in France, savored his personal success. He knew that Vorontsov's Francophile tendencies would lead him quite naturally to win over Catherine, and probably even Elizabeth, to side with Louis XV.

With regard to Catherine, he was not mistaken: anything that went against the tastes of her husband seemed salutary to her; with Elizabeth, things were less clear. She sought savagely to keep her free will, to obey only her own instinct. Moreover, the early military successes bolstered her hopes. Showing more resolve than Apraxin, General Fermor seized Königsberg, besieged Kustrin, and was making progress in Pomerania. However, he was stopped outside of Zorndorf, in a battle that was so indecisive that both camps proclaimed victory. Certainly, the French victory in Crefeld, on the Rhine, by the count of Clermont, briefly dampened the Empress's optimism. But experience had taught her that this kind of risk is inevitable in war and that it would be disastrous for Russia to lay down its weapons at the first sign of failure. Suspecting her allies of being less adamant than she in their bellicose intentions, she even declared to the ambassador of Austria, Count Esterhazy, that she would fight until the end, even if she had to "sell all her diamonds and half her dresses."

According to the reports that Elizabeth received from the theater of operations, this patriotic disposition was shared by all the soldiers, of high rank or low. In the palaces, on the other hand, opinions were less certain. It was considered proper, in some Russian circles associated with the embassies, to show a certain independence of mind in this respect; this was considered having a "European" outlook. The mindset promulgated in foreign capitals and bolstered by international alliances between great families encouraged an elegant and tolerant lifestyle straddling several borders, so that certain courtiers scoffed at those who only wished for a solution that would be fundamentally Russian. First among the partisans of Frederick II was, as always, the Grand Duke Peter, who no longer hid his cards. He claimed to be communicating to the king of Prussia (through the intermediary of England's new ambassador to St. Petersburg, George Keith, who had succeeded Williams) everything that the tsarina was saying in her secret war councils. Elizabeth did not want to believe that her nephew was receiving money as a price for his treason; but she was informed that Keith had received from his minister, Pitt (who also idolized the king of Prussia), instructions to encourage the grand duke to use all his influence with the empress to spare Frederick II from disaster.

Once upon a time, the Germanophiles could also count on Catherine and Poniatowski to support them. But, after the open-hearted conversation that she had had with her daughter-in-law, Elizabeth felt sure that she had definitively defeated her. Folding in on herself, retreating inward to simmer over her sentimental sorrows, the young woman now spent her time only weeping and dreaming. Since she had voluntarily removed herself from the game board, she had lost any importance on the international level. To ensure that she had been rendered harmless, Elizabeth dispatched Stanislaw Poniatowski on a foreign mission. Her Majesty then went one step further and, asking him to relinquish his passport, let him know that henceforth his presence in St. Petersburg would be deemed undesirable.

After having disarmed her daughter-in-law, the Empress thought that she had only to disarm one other adversary, who was hateful in a different way: Frederick II. She was set against the king of Prussia not only because he opposed her personal political views, but even more so because he had won over the heart of too many Russians, who were blinded by his insolence and his gleaming armor. Fortunately, Maria Theresa seemed as resolved as she to destroy the Germanic hegemony, and Louis XV, at the urging of Pompadour, it was said, was now engaging to reinforce the army he had launched against Frederick II's troops. On December 30, 1759, a third treaty of Versailles renewed the second and guaranteed to Austria the restitution of all the territories that had been occupied during preceding campaigns. That should be enough, thought Elizabeth, to revive the allies' flagging energies.

In parallel to all this official business, she conducted (with an almost youthful delight) a friendly correspondence with the king of France. The letters between the two monarchs were written by their respective secretaries, but the tsarina liked to think that those from Louis XV were really dictated by him and that the solicitude expressed in the letters was the sign of a genuine autumnal flirtation. Elizabeth was suffering from open wounds on her legs, and Louis XV stretched his compassion as far as to send her his personal surgeon, Dr. Poissonier. Certainly, it was not his skill with the scalpel and his ability to prescribe medications, but his capacity to collect information and to weave intrigues that had earned Poissonier the king's high regard. Having been invested with this secret mission, he was welcomed as an intelligence specialist by the Marquis de l'Hôpital. The ambassador counted on him to relieve the tsarina of her scruples, after having relieved her of her ulcers. One doctor is as good as another; why not provide Her Majesty with a second Lestocq?

However, as much as she trusted in Dr. Poissonier's curative science, Elizabeth resisted allowing him to guide her in her political decisions. The French were now proposing to land a Russian expeditionary force in Scotland in order to attack the English on their home territory, while the French fleet would meet the enemy in a naval action; Elizabeth considered the plan too hazardous and preferred to restrict her troops to land-based actions against Prussia.

Unfortunately, General Fermor had even less fight in him than the late Field Marshal Apraxin. Instead of leading the charge, he was marching in place, waiting at the borders of Bohemia for the arrival of hypothetical Austrian reinforcements. Annoyed by these delays, the Empress relieved Fermor and replaced him with Peter Saltykov, an old general who had spent his entire career in the Ukrainian militia. Known for his timidity, his weak appearance and his white militiaman's uniform (of which he was very proud), Peter Saltykov made a poor impression on the troops, who called him *Kurochka* (the Pullet) behind his back. However, from the very first engagement, the "pullet" turned out to be more combative than a cock. Taking advantage of a tactical error by Frederick II, Saltykov boldly moved toward Frankfurt. He had given notice to the Austrian regiment under General Gédéon de Laudon to meet him at the Oder. As soon as they met up, the road to Berlin would be open.

Frederick II, alerted to this threat against his capital, hastily returned from the depths of Saxony. Learning from his spies that his adversary's commanders, the Russian Saltykov and the Austrian Laudon, had fallen into dispute, he decided to take advantage of this dissension to launch a final attack. During the night of August 10, he crossed the Oder and advanced on the Russians, who were cut off in Kunersdorf. However, the Prussians' slow maneuvering deprived them of any benefit of surprise, and Laudon and Saltykov had time to reorganize their troops. Nonetheless, the battle was so violent and confused that Saltykov, in a flourish of theatricality, threw himself to his knees before his soldiers and beseeched "the god of Armies" to give them victory.

In fact, the decision was dictated by the Russian artillery, which had remained intact despite repeated attacks. On August 13, the Prussian infantry and then the cavalry were crushed by cannon shot. The survivors were overcome by panic. Of the 48,000 men originally commanded by Frederick II, only 3000 remained. This horde, exhausted and demoralized, was barely able to keep together a rearguard during its retreat. Overwhelmed by this defeat, Frederick II wrote to his brother: "The downstream effects of the matter are worse than the matter itself. I have no more resources. All is lost. I will not survive the loss of the fatherland!"

In giving his account of this victory to the tsarina, Saltykov showed himself more circumspect: "Your Imperial Majesty should not be surprised by our losses," he wrote, "for she is not unaware that the king of Prussia sells his defeats dearly. Another victory like this one, Majesty, and I will see myself constrained to walk to St. Petersburg, staff in hand, to bring you the news myself — for I will have no one else left to serve as courier."[3] Thoroughly reassured as to the outcome of the war, Elizabeth ordered "a *real* Te Deum" to be celebrated this time, and she declared to the Marquis de l'Hôpital: "Every good Russian must be a good Frenchman, and every good Frenchman must be a good Russian."[4]

As a reward for this great feat of arms, old Saltykov, "the Pullet," received the title of Field Marshal. Did this honor go to his head? Instead of pursuing the enemy in his retreat, he fell asleep on his laurels. All of Russia seemed to fall into a happy torpor at the idea of having demolished a leader as prestigious as Frederick II.

After a brief moment of despair, the Grand Duke Peter went back to believing in the German miracle. As for Elizabeth, dazed by the hymns, the artillery salvos, the ringing bells and the diplomatic congratulations, finally was delighted to be able to pause and reflect. Her bellicose temper was followed by a gradual return to reason: what harm would it do to allow Frederick II, having been taught a good lesson, to stay on his throne for a while? The main objective, surely, was to conclude an arrangement that was acceptable to all parties. But alas! it seems that France, at one time disposed to listen to the tsarina's concerns, returned to its old protectionist ways and recoiled at the thought of leaving her with a free hand in Eastern Prussia and Poland. One would almost think that Louis XV and his advisers, who had so ardently sought her assistance against Prussia and England, now feared that she would take too large a role in the European game, should victory be theirs.

To back up the Marquis de l'Hôpital, who was getting a bit old and tired, Versailles appointed the young baron of Breteuil. He arrived in St. Petersburg, all full of life. He was charged by the duke of Choiseul with convincing the Empress to delay further military operations in order not to "increase the embarrassments of the king of Prussia," since that could compromise the signing of a peace accord. At least, that is what the French envoy in Elizabeth's entourage was told. She was shocked by this call for moderation at the very hour when the spoils were to be divided. In front of Ambassador Esterhazy who, in the name of the Austro-Russian alliance, accused General Peter Saltykov of foot-dragging and thus helping England (whom he hinted might be paying for this indirect assistance), she flushed red with indignation and exclaimed: "We have never made a promise that we did not endeavor to hold ourselves to! . . . I will never allow that glory, bought at the price of the precious blood of our subjects, to be sullied by suspicions of insincerity!" And, in fact, at the end of the third year of a senseless war, she could say that Russia was the only power in the coalition that seemed ready to make every sacrifice to obtain the capitulation of Prussia.

Alexis Razumovsky supported her in her intransigence. He too had never ceased believing in the military and moral supremacy of the fatherland. However, when it came time to make the decisions to commit her troops in merciless combat, she consulted not her old lover, Alexis Razumovsky, not her current favorite, Ivan Shuvalov (so cultivated and so learned), nor her too-cautious and too-clever chancellor Mikhail Vorontsov, but the awesome memory of her grandfather, Peter the Great. It was he whom she had in mind on January 1, 1760, while everyone was making New Year's resolutions, when she publicly wished that her army would prove to be "more aggressive and more daring" in order to oblige Frederick II to submit. As a reward for this supreme effort, she stated that she would ask for nothing more than to take possession of Eastern Prussia, subject to a territorial exchange with Poland (which could, if need be, retain a semblance of autonomy). That last clause should be enough, she judged, to alleviate Louis XV's concerns.

To prepare for such delicate negotiations, the king of France rested his hopes on the assistance that the baron of Breteuil could lend to the aging marquis de l'Hôpital. In fact, it was not the baron's diplomatic experience that he counted on in circumventing the tsarina, but the seductive influence that the 27-year-old dandy seemed to have over women. Elizabeth knew the game too well not to see through Breteuil's false admiration of her glory; moreover, in analyzing his ploy, she understood that it was not she but the grand duchess whom he sought to allure into cooperating in furthering the interests of France. In order to win favor with Catherine, he offered her a choice — to allow him to make love to her as only a Frenchman knows how to do, or to persuade the tsarina to bring back Stanislaw Poniatowski, moldering as he was in his dull Poland. Whether she accepted either one of these offers or combined them both for her pleasure, she surely would be so grateful towards France that she would not be able to refuse him anything.

The time was right for such a charm offensive — especially given that the young woman had just suffered two serious heart-aches: the death of her daughter, young Anna,[5] and that of her mother, who had recently passed away in Paris. However, in spite of this twofold mourning, it happened that Catherine had finally overcome the depression that had held her back all these years and, better yet, she felt no need to take up again with her former lovers nor to entertain another one, even if he were French.

The truth is that she had not waited for the baron of Breteuil to come up with a successor to the men who used to brighten her days. Her newly-anointed had the unique qualities of being of purely Russian blood and a superb, well-built man, athletic, brash, and deep in debt, renowned for his escapades and ready to undertake any folly to protect his mistress. This was Grigory Or-lov. He and his four brothers all served in the imperial guard. His dedication to the traditions of his regiment reinforced his hatred of the Grand Duke Peter, who was well known for his contempt of the Russian army and its leaders. The very idea of this histri-onic poltroon swaggering about in a Holstein uniform, a self-proclaimed follower of Frederick II despite being heir to the throne of Russia, left Orlov feeling morally obliged to defend the grand duchess against her husband's irrational maneuvers.

Although exhausted by disease, age, political concerns and excesses of food and drink, the tsarina kept abreast of these devel-opments. She viewed her daughter-in-law's escapades with a mixture of reprobation and envy. She approved the deception for, in her opinion, the Grand Duke Peter deserved to be betrayed by his wife a hundred times over, having himself betrayed Russia with Prussia. But she was afraid that, by diverting the course of events, Catherine might prevent the realization of her dearest wish: the peaceful transfer of power, over the head of Peter, to his son, young Paul, who would be assisted by a regency council.

Admittedly, Elizabeth could have proclaimed this change in the dynastic order, right then. However, such an initiative inevitably would have entailed skirmishes between rival factions, revolts within the family and perhaps in the street. Wouldn't it be better to leave things as they were, for the time being? There was no need to rush; Her Majesty still had a clear head; she might live on a few more years; the country needed her; her subjects would not understand her suddenly ignoring current issues to deal with the succession.

As though to encourage her in maintaining the status quo, the "Conference," the supreme political council created at her initiative, was considering a march on Berlin by the combined allied armies. However, Field Marshal Saltykov being ill, General Fermor hesitated at the idea of such a large-scale action. Then, in a daring move, the Russian general Totleben launched an attack on the Prussian capital, surprised the enemy, penetrated the city and accepted its surrender. Although this "raid" was too fast and too poorly exploited to lead Frederick II to give up his entire territory, the king was sufficiently shaken that one might reasonably expect the ensuing negotiations to be highly profitable.

In such a context, Elizabeth felt that France should set an example of firmness. Ivan Shuvalov was so much persuaded of that, that his mistress would laugh and say that he was more French than the French. In addition, she believed that Catherine was on good terms with the baron of Breteuil only insofar as the politics of France did not contradict too directly that of Russia.

However, Breteuil, obeying his principal, the duke of Choiseul, advised the tsarina that Louis XV would be grateful to her if, exceptionally, she would agree to sacrifice "her particular interests to the common cause." In short, he asked her to settle for a compromise. But, in spite of the illness that kept her confined to her room, Elizabeth refused to let go before she received assurances that Russia would receive its due. In her view, prolonging the truce would only help Frederick II. She understood him well enough to know that he would take advantage of the suspension of hostilities to rebuild his army and to prepare to fight again, with a new chance of success. The Empress's mistrust and vindictiveness being abruptly awaked, she took the bit in her teeth. On her deathbed, she wanted to ensure that Russia would live on after her — and thanks to her. While in her shadow hushed rumors on the future of monarchy were circulating again, she and her advisers from the Conference were planning to attack Silesia and Saxony. As a final inspiration she named Alexander Buturlin commander-in-chief; his principal qualification for the position was that he had once been her lover.

While the *generalissimo*, appointed *in extremis*, was certainly full of good intentions, he had neither the authority nor the military knowledge necessary to fill the role. However, nobody in Elizabeth's inner circle warned her against the risks of such a choice. For one Ivan Shuvalov (who was always preaching all-out war), how many worthy advisers showed themselves strangely hesitant, inexplicably evasive!

Little by little, Elizabeth noted that even within the palace there were two irreconcilable political views, two groups of partisans who fought with arguments, tricks and intrigues. Some pushed for complete conquest for love of country; the others, tired of a war that was costly in terms of lives and money, wished to see it ended as soon as possible, even at the price of some concessions. Torn between the two camps, Elizabeth was almost ready to give up her claims on Eastern Prussia provided that France supported her claims on Polish Ukraine. In St. Petersburg, in London, in Vienna, and in Versailles, the diplomats haggled endlessly. That was their pleasure and their trade. But Elizabeth was wary of their quibbles. Even as everyone around her was discussing her health, she intended to keep a tight grip on the destiny of her empire, as long as she had the strength to read her mail and say her prayers. At times, she regretted being an old woman and unable, in that condition, to command her regiments in person.

In reality, in spite of the shifting winds in war and politics, things were not going so badly for Russia. These disturbing events ruffled the surface of the water, but deeper down, a strong current was flowing right along, maintained by the usual paper-pushing in the state offices, the harvests at the agricultural estates, the output of the factories, artisans' workshops and public building sites, and the comings and goings of boats in the ports and caravans in the steppes, bringing their cargos of exotic goods. This quiet agitation went on, like an anthill, in spite of the tumult at the top; and Elizabeth interpreted it as a sign of the extraordinary vitality of her people. Come what may, she thought, Russia is so vast, so rich in good land and courageous men that it can never perish. If one could cure it of its subservience to Prussian models, the game would be half-won already. For her part, she could take pride in having, in just a few years' time, removed most of the Germans who had run the Administration. Whenever her advisers had suggested a foreigner for an important position, her invariable answer was, "Don't we have a Russian to put there?" This systematic preference quickly became known to her subjects and led to the arrival of new statesmen and military men, eager to devote themselves to the service of the empire.

While bringing new blood into the hierarchy of civil servants, the empress had also set about boosting the country's economy by removing the internal customs system, instituting banks of credit like those in other European states, encouraging the colonization of the uncultivated plains of the southwest, creating the first secondary schools here and there, and founding the university in Moscow (to succeed the Slavo-Greco-Latin Academy in that city) and the Academy of Sciences in St. Petersburg. Thus she maintained, against all the winds and tides, the trend of opening to the Western culture that Peter the Great had so urgently fostered, and without too much sacrificing the land's traditions that were so cherished by the old nobility. While she recognized the defects of serfdom, she by no means planned to give up this secular practice. Let unrepentant utopians dream of a paradise where rich and poor, *muzhiks* and landowners, illiterate and erudite, blind and clear-sighted, young and old, minstrels and freaks would all have the same chance in life — she was too conscious of the harsh Russian reality to subscribe to such a mirage. On the other hand, whenever she found, within reach, an opportunity to extend the geographical limits of Russia, she became possessed, like a gambler at a betting table.

At the end of 1761, just when she was starting to doubt the abilities of her military chiefs, the fortress of Kolberg (in Pomerania) fell into the hands of the Russians. The attack was led by Rumiantsev, with a promising new general at his side — one Alexander Suvorov. This unhoped-for victory proved the empress right in holding out against the skeptics and the defeatists.

However, she hardly had the strength to enjoy the moment. She had just spent a few weeks resting at Peterhof, but it had not brought her any relief. Returning to the capital, the satisfaction brought by her country's military victory was soon effaced by the turmoil around her. She was haunted by the thought of death and caught up in rumors of dynastic intrigues, the grand duchess's love scandals and the grand duke's stupid, stubborn obsession with the triumph of Prussia. Shut up in her room, she suffered most of all from her legs, whose wounds bled in spite of every remedy. Moreover, she was becoming prone to hemorrhages and crises of hysteria, which left her dazed for hours. Now, she would receive her ministers sitting up in bed, her hair capped with a lace bonnet. Sometimes, to cheer herself up, she would call in the mimes from an Italian troupe that she had invited to St. Petersburg; she would watch their pranks and think back to the time when such buffoons used to make her laugh.

As soon as she felt a little more puckish, she asked to have some of her most beautiful dresses brought in and, after pondering a bit, chose one; at the risk of splitting the seams, she had her chambermaids dress her, entrusted her coiffure to the hairdresser with instructions to give her the latest Parisian fashion, and announced her intention to appear at the next court ball. Then, planted in front of a mirror, she lost heart at the sight of her wrinkles, her sagging eyelids, her triple chin and the blotches on her cheeks; she had herself undressed, went back to bed, and resigned herself to ending her life in solitude, lethargy and memories. Greeting the rare courtiers who came to visit her, she read in their eyes a suspicious curiosity, the cold impatience of the lookout on a watchtower. They may have had an affectionate look on their faces, but they weren't coming to wish her well — they wanted to see how long she had left to live. Only Alexis Razumovsky seemed to really care. But what was he thinking about, as he looked at her? Of the loving and demanding woman whom he had held so often in his arms, or of the corpse that he would soon be strewing with flowers?

To the disastrous obsession with death, Elizabeth soon added a fear of fire. The old Winter Palace where the tsarina had lived in St. Petersburg since the beginning of her reign was an immense wooden construction that, at the least spark, would go up like a torch. If fire broke out in some recess of her apartments, she would lose all her furniture, all her holy images, all her dresses.

And she would certainly not have time to escape, herself, but would perish in a blazing hell. Such disasters were, after all, frequent in the capital. She would have to summon up the courage to relocate. But to where? The construction of the new palace, which Elizabeth had entrusted to Rastrelli, was so far behind schedule that one could not hope to see an end to the work in less than two or three years. The Italian architect was asking for 380,000 rubles just to finish Her Majesty's private apartments. She did not have that kind of money, and she did not know where to find it. Maintaining the army was costing an arm and a leg. Moreover, in June 1761, a fire had devastated the hemp and flax depots, destroying valuable goods that would have been sold to help replenish the State coffers.

To console herself for this penury and this typically Russian chaos, the tsarina went back to drinking great quantities of alcohol. When she had downed enough glasses, she would collapse in bed, sleeping like a beast. Her chambermaids watched over her while she rested; and she kept a special watchman, in addition — the *spalnik*, who was charged with checking her breathing, listening to her complaints and calming her fears whenever she began to wake up, between blackouts. To this good man, uneducated, naive and humble as a domestic animal, she no doubt entrusted the concerns that beset her as soon as she closed her eyes. All the family troubles simmered in her head together with the political intricacies, making an unpalatable stew. Chewing over old resentments and vain illusions, she hoped that at least death would hold off until she signed a final agreement with the king of France. That Louis XV should have spurned her as a fiancée when she was only fourteen years old and he was fifteen, she could (if need be) understand. But that he should hesitate now to recognize her as a unique and faithful ally, when they were both at the height of their glory, surpassed understanding. That rogue, Frederick II,

rovna sleeps in the peace of the Lord," adding the consecrated formula, "She has commanded to us to live long." Lastly, in his powerful voice, doing away with any possible ambiguity, he said, "God keep our Very Gracious Sovereign, the Emperor Peter III."

After the death of Elizabeth "the Lenient," her associates piously inventoried her wardrobes and trunks. They found 15,000 dresses, some of which Her Majesty had never worn.

The first to bow down before the trimmed and made-up corpse were, as expected, her nephew Peter III (who found it difficult to disguise his joy) and her daughter-in-law Catherine (already preoccupied with how to play this new hand of cards). The cadaver, embalmed, scented, hands crossed and head crowned, remained on exhibit for six weeks in a room in the Winter Palace. Among the crowd that filed past the open casket, many unknown individuals wept for Her Majesty who had so loved the ordinary people and who had not hesitated to punish the faults of the mighty. But the visitors irresistibly shifted their gaze from the impassive mask of the tsarina to the pale and serious face of the grand duchess, who knelt by the catafalque. Catherine seemed to have sunk into a never-ending prayer. Actually, while she may have been murmuring interminable prayers, she must in fact have been thinking about how to conduct herself in the future, to thwart the hostility of her husband.

The presentation of the late empress to the people, in the palace, was followed by the transfer of the remains to the Cathedral of Our Lady of Kazan. There again, during the religious ceremonies (which lasted ten days), Catherine astonished those in attendance by her demonstrations of grief and piety. Was she trying to prove how Russian she was, whereas her husband, the Grand Duke Peter, never missed an occasion to show that he was not? While the coffin was being solemnly transported from the Kazan Cathedral to that of the Peter and Paul Fortress, for burial in the crypt reserved for sovereigns of Russia, the new tsar scandalized the most enlightened minds by laughing and making faces behind the hearse. He must have been taking his revenge for all the past humiliations by thumbing his nose at the dead. But no one laughed at his high-jinks on a day of national mourning.

Covertly watching her husband, Catherine realized that he was contributing to his own undoing. Moreover, he very quickly announced the color of his intentions. The night following his accession, he gave the order for Russian troops immediately to evacuate the territories that they occupied in Prussia and Pomerania. At the same time, he offered to sign "an accord of eternal peace and friendship" with Frederick II, who had been conquered only yesterday. Blinded by his admiration for this prestigious enemy, he threatened to impose the Holstein uniform on the Russian imperial guard, to disband in a flourish of the quill certain regiments that he considered too devoted to the dear departed, and to make the Orthodox Church toe the line by obliging the priests to shave their beards and to wear frock coats like Protestant pastors.

His Germanophilia took such proportions that Catherine was afraid he would soon repudiate her and lock her up in a convent. However, her partisans told her repeatedly that she had all of Russia behind her — and that the imperial guard would not tolerate anyone touching a hair on her head. The five Orlov brothers, led by her lover Grigory, persuaded her that, far from despairing, she should be delighted by the turn of events. It was time to play all-out, they said. Didn't Catherine I, Anna Ivanovna, and Elizabeth I all win the throne through coups of outrageous audacity? The first three empresses of Russia had shown her the way. Now, she only had follow in their footsteps.

On June 28, 1762, the very same day that the Baron of Breteuil wrote in a dispatch to his government that, "a public cry of dissatisfaction is going up [in Russia]," Catherine, escorted by

Alexis Orlov, went to visit the Guard regiments. She went from one barrack to another and was hailed enthusiastically everywhere. The supreme consecration was given to her at once at Our Lady of Kazan, where the priests, who knew her by her so-often displayed piety, blessed her for her imperial destiny. The following day, riding (in an officer's uniform) at the head of several regiments who had joined her cause, she moved on to Oranienbaum where her husband, who suspected nothing, was regaling himself in the company of his mistress, Elizabeth Vorontsov. He was stunned to receive an emissary from his wife and to hear, from his mouth, that a military uprising has just driven him out.

His Holstein troops not having managed to offer any resistance to the insurgent, he signed, sobbing and trembling with fear, the act of abdication that was presented to him. At that, Catherine's partisans packed him off in a closed carriage to the palace of Ropcha, some thirty versts from St. Petersburg, where he was placed under house arrest.

Catherine returned to St. Petersburg on Sunday, June 30, 1762, and was greeted by the peeling carillon of church bells, salvos of artillery fire and howls of joy.[6] It seemed that Russia was delighted to be become Russian again, thanks to her. Was it reassuring to the people to find another woman at the helm? In the sequence of the dynastic succession, she would be the fifth, after Catherine I, Anna Ivanovna, Anna Leopoldovna and Elizabeth I (Petrovna) to ascend the steps of the throne. Who then could claim that the skirt impedes the natural movements of a woman? Never had Catherine felt more at ease nor more sure of herself. Those who had preceded her in this difficult role had given her courage and a kind of legitimacy. It was brains, not sex, that was now the best asset for achieving power.

However, six days after her entry in St. Petersburg in apotheosis, Catherine received a letter from an extremely embarrassed Alexis Orlov, stating that Peter III had been mortally wounded during a brawl with his guards at Ropcha. She was thunderstruck. Wouldn't the people blame her for this brutal and suspicious death? Wouldn't all those who had cheered her so vigorously yesterday in the streets rather come to hate her for a crime that she did not commit, but that indeed suited her interests very well? The next day, she was relieved — no one was upset at the death of Peter III, and no one thought of implicating her in such a necessary development. Indeed, this murder that reviled her seemed rather to answer to the wishes of the nation.

Some in her entourage had been present during the accession of another Catherine, in 1725. They could not be prevented from thinking that in the past 37 years, four women had occupied the throne of Russia: the Empresses Catherine I, Anna Ivanovna and Elizabeth I, with the short interlude of a regency led by Anna Leopoldovna. How could the survivors be kept from drawing comparisons between the different sovereigns? The oldest among them cited odd similarities between these female autocrats. In Catherine I, Anna Ivanovna and Anna Leopoldovna, they detected the same lubricity, the same surfeits of pleasure and cruelty, the same taste for buffoonery and ugliness, combined with the same quest for luxury and the same need to throw dust in people's eyes. This primitive frenzy and this fundamental egoism were also found in Elizabeth, but moderated by her concern to appear "lenient," in accordance with the nickname given her by the people. Admittedly, for those who were familiar with the court, each of these extreme personalities was distinguished by a hundred other characteristics; but, for anyone who had not been closely involved, they all became confused. Was it Catherine I, or Anna Leopoldovna, or Anna Ivanovna, or Elizabeth I who had dreamt up that wedding night of the two buffoons locked in an ice palace? Which of those omnipotent ogresses had taken a Cossack as her lover, the cantor of the imperial chapel? Which of the four enjoyed the clowning of her dwarves as much as the groans of the prisoners put to torture? Which one had combined, with an omnivorous greed, the pleasures of the flesh and those of political action? Which of them had been a good person but indulged her vilest instincts, pious while offending God at every step? Which of them, although barely literate, opened a university in Moscow and made it possible for Lomonosov to lay the bases of the modern Russian language? For the flabbergasted contemporaries, during this period, it seemed that there had been only one tyrannical and sensual woman, not three tsarinas and a regent, who inaugurated the era of the matriarchy in Russia under different faces and names.

Perhaps it is because she loved men so much that Elizabeth so much liked to dominate them. And they, eternal fire-eaters, were happy to feel her heel on the back of their necks, and they even asked for more! Reflecting on the fates of her famous predecessors, Catherine must have thought that the ability to adopt a masculine mindset when it came to politics and to be physically feminine in bed was the outstanding characteristic of all her congenerics, as soon as they felt the inkling of an opinion on state affairs. The exercise of autocracy, rather than blunting their sensuality, exacerbated it. The more they assumed responsibility for leading the nation, the more they felt the need to appease their reproductive instincts that had to be set aside during the tedious administrative discussions. Wasn't that proof of the original ambivalence of woman, whose vocations were surely not only pleasure and procreation but who was also exercising her legitimate role when determining the destiny of a people? Suddenly, Catherine was dazzled by the evidence of history: more than any other nation, Russia was the empire of women. She dreamed to model it to match her ideal, to polish it without distorting it.

From the first Catherine to the second, the morals of the land had imperceptibly evolved. The robust oriental cruelty had already given way, in the salons, to false airs of European culture. The new tsarina was determined to encourage that metamorphosis. But her next ambition was to make everyone forget her Germanic origins, her German accent, her former name of Sophia of Anhalt-Zerbst, and to have all the Russians accept her as the most Russian of sovereigns, the Empress Catherine II of Russia. She was 33 years old, and had her whole life before her to prove her merit. And that is more than one needs when one has, as she had, faith in one's own star and in one's country. What difference did it make that this wasn't her country by birth — it was her country by choice. What could be more noble, she thought, than to build a future independent of the concepts of nationality and genealogy? And isn't that why she would one day be known as Catherine the Great?

Footnotes

1. The details of this meeting and the remarks that were exchanged were recorded by Catherine II in her *Mémoires*. Cf. Henri Troyat, *op. cit.*
2. *Ibid.*
3. Cf. K. Waliszewski, *op. cit.*
4. Cf. Daria Olivier, *op. cit.*
5. Anna died at the age of three months, on March 19, 1759.
6. For a detailed account of these and other critical moments, see, among others, Henri Troyat, *op. cit.*

INDEX

THE ROMANOV DYNASTY

Mikhail (1596–1645)
Tsar from 1613 to 1645
m. 1624 Princess Maria Dolgoruky († 1625),
Then m. 1626 Eudoxia Streshchev (1608–1645)

Alexis, called the Peaceful Tsar (1629–1676)
Tsar from 1645 to 1676
M. 1648 Maria Miloslawskievna (1629–1669),
Then m. 1671 Natalya Naryshkin (1651–1694)

From the first marriage:
Fyodor III (1661–1682)
Tsar from 1676 to 1682
m. in 1680
Agrafiya Gruchevsky
(1665–1681),
then in 1682 Marfa Apraxin
(1664–1716)
|
Ilya, b. and d. 1681
(from the first marriage)

Sophia (1657–1704)
Regent from 1682 to 1689,
then retired to a convent

Ivan V, called the Simple
(1666–1696)
Tsar from 1682 to 1696
with Peter the Great
m. in 1684
Praskovya Soltikov
(1664–1723)

From the second marriage:
Peter I, called the Great
(1672–1725)
Tsar from 1682 to 1725
m. in 1689
Eudoxia Lapukhin
(1682–1727),
then in 1707
Catherine Skavronska
(future **Catherine I**)
Empress from 1725–1727

Catherine (1691-1733)
m. in 1716
Charles Leopold
of Mecklenburg
(1678-1747)

Anna Ivanovna
(1693-1740)
Tsarina from 1730 to 1740
m. in 1710
Duke Frederick William
of Courland (1692-1711)

Praskovya (1694-1731)
m. Ivan Marmonov

Elizabeth Petrovna
(1709-1762)
Empress from 1741 to 1762
m. 1742 (in secret)
Alexis Razumovsky
(1709-1771)

From the first marriage:
Alexis (1690-1718)
Tsarevich
m. Charlotte
of Brunswick
(1694-1715)

From the second marriage:
Anna Petrovna
(1708-1728)
m. in 1725
Duke Charles Frederick
of Holstein-Gottorp

Peter II (1715-1730)
Tsar from 1727 to 1730

Peter III (1728-1762)
né Charles Peter Ulrich
of Holstein-Gottorp
Tsar in 1762
m. in 1745
Sophia of Anhalt-Zerbst (1729-1796),
future **Catherine II**, called the Great,
Empress from 1762 to 1796

Anna Leopoldovna
(1718-1746)
m. in 1739
Anthony Ulrich
of Brunswick (1714-1774)
Regent 1740-1741

Ivan VI (1740-1764)
Tsar from 1740 to 1741